STEWARDSHIP

MINISTRIES

Published by Stewardship Ministries
© Copyright 2011. All Rights Reserved.

Requests for permission should be addressed in writing to: Stewardship Ministries, 5237 State Rd. 144 Mooresville, IN 46158.

This study guide is the text for the Life Stewardship Study Series.

Unless otherwise noted, all Scripture quotations are from the Holy Bible New International Version © Copyright 1973, 1978, 1984 by International Bible Society.

To order additional copies of this study guide, visit www.stewardshipministries.org.

With grateful acknowledgment to Scott Titus and his team at InsideOUT for their partnership in ministry and excellent work in bringing this project to life.

Life Stewardship Series

Series #1: Introduction: The Meaning of Stewardship

Week #1

Week #2

Week #3

Series #2: The Examined Life of a Good and Faithful Steward

Week #4

Week #5

Concluding Lesson: The Rewarded Life of a Good and Faithful Steward

The Concept of a Steward

What Is My Relationship to My Stuff?

This is clearly the most foundational question we must answer if we are goin to make any progress in our attitudes, perspectives, and decisions in relatio material things—particularly material wealth. If we cannot answer this quest clarity and confidence, we will find ourselves—in spite of our financial succe underachieving in our lives. If you think of this question as a stool with three upon which the answer is balanced, you will be able to better envision the t about your stuff.

Leg #1

The first "leg" of this stool is the fact that God owns everything because He created everything. King David tells us in Psalm 24:1, "The earth is the Lord's and all it contains, the world, and those who dwell in it." He goes on to add in Psalm 50:10-12 cev,

> *Every animal in the forest belongs to me, and so do the cattle on a thousand hills.*
> *I know all the birds in the mountains,*
> *and every wild creature is in my care.*
> *If I were hungry, I wouldn't tell you,*
> *because I own the world and everything in it.*

Not only did God create everything that exists, He used all of His own materials to build it. So He truly is the only One who can claim to own anything.

If we build something, we may claim it is ours, but if we use someone else's materials to build it, then the owner of those materials can lay some claim to it as well. But in God's case, He not only dreamed it all u used His own creative materials to build it.

Leg #2

The second "leg" of this stool is the fact that not only did God create us, but He also redeemed us from slavery to the prince of this world through the death of His son, Jesus Christ. Paul tells us in Titus 2:13b- "Christ Jesus, who gave Himself for us to redeem us from every lawless deed, and to purify for Himself a people for His own possession, zealous for good deeds."

This word redeem that Paul uses here is no longer commonly used in our culture today. When I was a yc boy it was used often. I remember going to the grocery store with my mother. At the checkout counter, s would be given a certain number of S&H Green Stamps depending on how large her grocery purchase was. The reason I remember this so well is because I was charged with the task of licking those "tasty" li stamps and then putting them into the books.

My mother had a catalog filled with all kinds of products—everything from small kitchen appliances to a c I was hoping my mother was not saving stamps for the car because it was several thousand Green Stam books. I could see my tongue being forever stuck to the roof of my mouth from licking that many stamps What made the Green Stamp catalog so unusual was that instead of having prices for each item, it had t umber of S&H Green Stamp books needed. A hand mixer might be four and a half books and a television 20 books. Do you remember the name of the place where you went to get these products? It was called ne Redemption Center. It was the place where you would take your Green Stamp books to redeem the em you wanted. In other words, you traded in your stamp books for something you wanted to own.

his is what God did with Jesus. God was willing to redeem us by offering the blood of His own Son, so e could again own us—"a people for His own possession." You see, God owns Christians twice—once ecause He made us and the second time because He bought us back after we were lost.

ne last thought on this leg: What was the reason Paul gave in Titus 2:14 for why God was willing to edeem us? It was so we could be "zealous for good deeds." Keep that thought in mind as we will be iscussing this later in the book.

eg #3

he final "leg" is the fact that we own nothing. We are called by God to be stewards, carrying out the Owner's wishes for His property. It is at this point that we need to come to grips with the terribly misused nd abused concept of stewardship.

efore I focus on what stewardship does mean, let me tell you what it does not mean. Churches routinely se the term stewardship to refer to their capital campaigns. These campaigns are simply fundraisers used o get church members to give. But since "fundraiser" has such a negative connotation, they substitute ncorrectly) the seemingly nobler phrase "stewardship drive."

ou will often hear churches and pastors use stewardship as a synonym for tithing. I have seen in many hurch papers and bulletins the term stewardship used as a heading to report the weekly offerings and ttendance. All of these uses that link stewardship to giving and tithing are inadequate at best—and ntirely wrong at worst.

y definition, a steward is "a person who manages another's property or financial affairs; one who dministers anything as the agent of another or others, a manager." So, for us to be "stewards for God," ve must acknowledge that all we are and all we have possession of belongs to Him. We are charged with nanaging His property according to His wishes.

ou can see that stewardship is not at all a synonym for tithing and fundraising; it is actually the opposite. Tithing has to do with what you give; stewardship has to do with what you keep. In other words, it is about now you manage everything that you have been entrusted to oversee. What most people miss is that stewardship is more about how you manage what is left over after you give than it is about what you give.

he radical, biblical concept of stewardship is easy enough to understand intellectually. However, it is nything but easy to consistently apply and live out. So what is your relationship to your stuff? You are not he owner; you are merely the caretaker of somebody else's property. And it is your job to manage all of it according to the Owner's wishes. Now, that really changes the game, does it not?

The Concept of a Steward

Life Application Questions

1. What is your initial reaction to this video?

_____

_____

_____

_____

2. Take a couple of minutes and create a personal balance sheet of all you own (Do not put any valu
with them, even if you can - just a description of the assets.) What is on your balance sheet?

_____

_____

_____

_____

3. Look again at what Psalm 24:1 and Psalm 50:10-12 say. Create your personal balance sheet aga

_____

_____

_____

_____

4. Why is it so important to acknowledge and accept that we are only managers of God's possessio
and not the owners of them? Practically speaking, what difference does it make in how we think
and how we live?

_____

_____

_____

_____

5. What has been your current understanding of the word *stewardship* prior to this lesson? In what ways have you heard it used, taught and/or preached in a Christian context?

_____

_____

_____

_____

6. What would happen to a manager of a store if he/she ignored or refused to follow the directions given to him/her by the owner of that store?

_____

_____

_____

_____

7. What might your answer to the above question mean to how you are stewarding the "store" that the Lord has given you to manage?

_____

_____

_____

_____

The Concept of a Steward

Keeping the Heart of God at the Heart of Living

I can think of no better way to define what stewardship really is than with the phrase—keeping the heart of God at the heart of living. Stewardship is all about carrying out the wishes of the Owner. The Owner is God and we are merely the caretakers of His property. Psalm 24:1 states it clearly, "The earth is the Lord's and all it contains, the world and all who live in it." I think this encompasses everything we will ever get our hands on in this lifetime.

This concept of stewardship is critically important, yet so often misunderstood. Even those who intellectually acknowledge that God owns everything do not functionally live as though He does. Let me illustrate my point by asking you to choose which one of the three questions below is the question we should be asking in regards to our material possessions.

1. What do I want to do with all my possessions?

2. What do I want to do with God's possessions?

3. What does God want me to do with His possessions?

No doubt you chose #3 as the proper question. In about thirty years of asking this question, every believer chooses #3. Intellectually, everyone is able to get this part of it. But practically speaking, we live as though #2 was the right question. We are more than happy to acknowledge that it all belongs to God, but when it comes to making decisions about what to do with what we oversee, we seldom, if ever, seek direction from the Owner.

Let me offer a few simple questions that should demonstrate just how true this is.

• When you bought your last car, did you ask God if this is the car He wanted you to buy with His money?

• When your money manager proposed an investment portfolio for you, did you go to the Lord and ask Him if these were the places He wanted His money invested?

• The last time you went shopping for clothes, did you ask your Father if these were the clothes He wanted you to wear?

• Did we check with God to see if He wanted us to over-indulge His dwelling place with that last meal?

I hope you see my point. We are all routinely guilty of intellectually acknowledging that God owns everything, while we live, spend, and invest like it is all our own. The cornerstone of stewardship is full acknowledgment and consistent practice of allowing God to direct what He wants done with what He has entrusted us to manage.

have recently been struck quite seriously with the reality that all our sin, at its core, is the result of personal selfishness. I would encourage you to ponder this yourself for a moment. As I have mulled this idea over and over in my mind, I have yet to find any exception. The truth is: we are our own worst enemies. We are continually getting in the way of God's best because we are so consumed with our desires, our rights, our dreams, our passions, and our way that we continually fall into sins of either commission (doing the wrong thing) or omission (not doing the right thing). Think about it. Why do we lie? Why do we cheat? Why do we steal? Why are we afraid? Why do we hate? Why do we commit adultery? Why do we lose our temper? Why do we become addicted to drugs, work, and entertainment? Why do we covet what others have? Why do we wear "masks" around others? Why do we not want to submit to God? I could go on and on, but it always circles back around to self. As the cartoon character Pogo confessed, "We have met the enemy and he is us."

The reason I am making this point is to say that our practical rejection of a life of devoted stewardship is just another example of how self gets in the way of God's best for us. We want to be in charge. We want to make the decisions. We want to "pull the trigger" and get things done. In ignoring the reality that we are nothing more than mere low-level managers who are expected to meticulously carry out the wishes of the all-loving and all-powerful Owner, our personal will, wishes, choices, and decisions prove to be categorically irrelevant to the discussion.

Someone once noted that at the center of SIN is the letter "I." We will always find "I"—self, ego, always looking out for number one—at the center of our sin.

- This is why Jesus said that if we really want to live, we must first die to self. "For whoever wants to save his life will lose it, but whoever loses his life for me will find it" (Matthew 16:25 niv).

- If you want to be first, you must let everyone else go ahead of you. As the scripture says, "The last will be first, and the first last" (Matthew 20:16 esv).

- If you want to be really free, you must submit to slavery. "Whoever wants to become great among you must be your servant, and whoever wants to be first must be your slave" (Matthew 20:26-27 niv).

- If you want to be great, you must strive to make everyone else greater than yourself. "Do nothing out of selfish ambition or vain conceit, but in humility consider others better than yourselves" (Philippians 2:3 niv, see also Luke 9:48).

It is all about death to self.

The reason stewardship is so challenging to practice is that we must get self out of the way. As long as we are fallen creatures with a fallen nature, we will have to wrestle daily with the lingering ghosts of our own selfishness until we someday finally shed this "dirt body" and move on to better things. In the mean time, we must resist with every ounce of our being the temptation to inappropriately assume the throne and play little gods over stuff that does not even belong to us.

The Concept of a Steward

Life Application Questions

1. What is your initial reaction to this video?

_____

_____

_____

_____

2. We were asked to choose which of these three stewardship questions was the right question to ask...

    1. What do I want to do with all my possessions?
    2. What do I want to do with God's possessions?
    3. What does God want me to do with His possessions?
    ...which one did you initially choose as the right stewardship question?

_____

_____

_____

_____

3. How have you seen an intellectual disconnect between knowing that question #3 is the right questi
and how you are currently living and handling your possessions?

_____

_____

_____

_____

4. Consider these three groups of people.

    1. Unbelievers
    2 Cultural Christians [people who have a "form of godliness, although they have denied its power," II Timothy 3:5]
    3. Sincere followers of Jesus

Which of these three questions (in question #2 above) would each group most likely ask?

_____

_____

_____

_____

Based upon what question you practically ask in your daily life, which of these three groups does it put you in?

_____

_____

_____

_____

5. How does your own sinfulness/selfishness cause you to "inappropriately assume the throne and play little gods over stuff that does not even belong to you?"

_____

_____

_____

_____

Has this been true in your life? If so, what are you going to do to change it? If not, how have you successfully avoided that temptation?

_____

_____

_____

_____

The Concept of a Steward

6. What would be the practical life-ramifications today if you were to formally and fully return everyth
you possess back to the rightful Owner from whom you have confiscated the ownership – not jus
your head, but in your heart?

_____

_____

_____

_____

What will be different in your life starting tomorrow if you were to return everything you possess ba
to God, the Owner?

_____

_____

_____

_____

How will your life change if you from this day forward seek to literally keep "the heart of God at the
heart of your living?"

_____

_____

_____

_____

The Concept of a Steward - Additional Food for Thought/Home Study Material

Resident Aliens

INTRODUCTION:

I would like for us to consider a very difficult concept. It is not a difficult concept to understand. But it is a difficult concept to consistently apply in our daily lives.

I want to talk to you about how you see yourself. But not in the way that has become so popular today. I do not want to talk to you about having a positive self–image or how you feel about yourself.

I want to look at this matter of worldview using a different focus and emphasis. I want to talk to you about your perception of how you and the world relate to one another and how your particular worldview translates into everyday life specifically in the areas of stewardship of your time, your talents, and your treasures.

It is interesting that in life a worldview is really no where formally taught. Unfortunately, for most people worldview is informally learned over a long period of time, constructed in much the same way that we put together a jig saw puzzle; one piece at a time until your "worldview" picture is complete and makes sense to you. And once your "worldview" picture is put together, your prevailing attitudes, your daily actions and your life goals will all be the direct result of the worldview you have assembled. I believe there are essentially three radically different worldviews – one of which is adopted by every human being on the face of this earth.

PROPOSITION:

Which of these three worldviews we adopt will lead us to totally contrary lifestyles and totally different destinies.

I. THE FIRST WORLDVIEW IS THAT OF A "NATIVE".

    A. What is a "NATIVE?"

        1. Romans 12:2 "Be not conformed to this WORLD"...

        2. "WORLD" is the Greek word "Cosmos" –"World" in the New Testament is not referring to a place (a planet). It is referring to a group of people. The word "Cosmos" means, "Those who are neutral to or opposed to God."

            a. So, it is not just those people like the late Madeline Murray-O'Hare, the ACLU, and many others who actively seek to dismantle Christianity and rid the planet of any evidence of it that are included in this definition.
            b. It may also be that nice person down the road who is morally upright and friendly, but has no time or interest in God or the things of God.

    c.   These people are what Paul calls the COSMOS. These people are the WORLD. These people are the NATIVES.

B. What is a "NATIVE'S" worldview?

    1. The Native says flatly, "This world is all that there is."

    2. That is why they want to...

        a.   save the whales
        b.   save the rain forest
        c.   save the darter snail
        d.   save the spotted owl.
        e.   save the environment
        f.   save our mother... the earth.

    3. They have slogans that reflect this worldview.

        a.   "You only go around once in life, so grab all the gusto you can"
        b.   "America, love it or leave it!"
        c.   "The one who dies with the most toys - wins." They miss one very important point. The one who dies with the most toys – still dies.
        d.   The Native lives solely for this life and what it provides.
        e.   The Native will "eat, drink and be merry, for tomorrow he will die."

I. THE SECOND WORLDVIEW IS THAT OF AN "ALIEN."

A. What is an "ALIEN?" "A foreigner that has gone to a foreign country for a purpose."

    1. It could be he is leaving something unpleasant behind in his homeland or he is looking forward to an opportunity in the land to which he is going.

    2. Aliens could be like the refugees from Kosovo, or the "boat people" from the Vietnam era.

    3. Aliens could also be like the immigrants from Ireland and Europe who migrated to this great land looking for a better opportunity for themselves and their families. This later purpose – aliens looking forward to an opportunity - best fits our topic here. An alien is a foreigner with a purpose. He has come to the new land with a purpose - on a mission if you will.

B. What is an "ALIEN'S" worldview?

The Concept of a Steward - Additional Food for Thought/Home Study Material

1. Within the spiritual context we are discussing here, an alien says, "I have been sent a specific mission by my homeland."

2. The Mission: Planetary domination. Domination not by force and power like the great conquering nations of the past, but planetary domination through gentleness, meekness, love and service.

3. The Goal: Convert individual Natives from citizenship of this world to citizenship in the next.

4. Every aspect of an Alien's life is directed towards accomplishing his Reigning Monarch's stated mission. He walks and talks and eats and sleeps and plans and works and sacrifices to fulfill his assigned purpose. Nothing sidetracks him from his mission.

5. The old spy movies provide a sense of the risk, sacrifice and dedication of carrying c their mission – often their "mission impossible."

6. And nothing in this world could entice an alien to forsake his allegiance to his homeland and its stated purpose and his commitment to fulfill that purpose.

C. There are literally dozens of Biblical examples of Aliens who refused to defect to the side of t Natives.

1. Moses - Hebrews 11:25-26

   "By faith Moses, when he had grown up, refused to be called the son of Pharaoh's daughter; choosing rather to endure ill-treatment with the people of God, than to enjoy the passing pleasures of sin..."

2. Shadrach, Meshach, Abednego - Daniel 3: 16-18

   "Shadrach, Meshach and Abednego answered and said, 'O Nebuchadnezzar, we do not need to give you an answer concerning this. If it be so, our God who we serve is able to deliver us out of your hand, O king. But even if He does not, let it be known to you, O king, that we are not going to serve your gods or worship the golden image that you have set up.'"

3. Peter and John before the Sanhedrin - Acts 3:18-21

   "And when they had summoned them, they commanded them not to speak or teach at all in the name of Jesus. But Peter and John answered and said to them, "Wheth it is right in the sight of God to give heed to you rather than to God, you be the judge for we cannot stop speaking what we have seen and heard."

4. In the days of the Roman Emperor Nero, a band of soldiers known as the Emperor's Wrestlers served him. They were picked from the best and the bravest of the land, recruited from the great athletes of the Roman amphitheater.

    In the great amphitheater they upheld the arms of the emperor against all challengers. Before each contest they stood before the emperor's throne. Then through the courts of Rome rang the cry: "We, the wrestlers, wrestling for thee, O Emperor, to win for thee the victory and free thee, the victor's crown."

    When the great Roman army was sent to fight in Gaul, no soldiers were braver or more loyal than this band of wrestlers led by their centurion Vespasian. But news reached Nero that many Roman soldiers had accepted the Christian faith. Therefore, this decree was dispatched to the centurion Vespasian; "If there be any among your soldiers who cling to the faith of the Christian, they must die!"

    The decree was received in the dead of winter. The soldiers were camped on the shore of a frozen inland lake. It was with sinking heart that Vespasian, the centurion, read the emperor's message.

    Vespasian called the soldiers together and asked: "Are there any among you who cling to the faith of the Christian? If so, let him step forward!" Forty wrestlers instantly stepped forward two paces, respectfully saluted, and stood at attention. Vespasian paused. He had not expected so many, nor such select ones. "Until sundown I shall await your answer," said Vespasian. Sundown came. Again the question was asked. Again the forty wrestlers stepped forward.

    Vespasian pleaded with them long and earnestly without prevailing upon a single man to deny his Lord. Finally he said, "The decree of the emperor must be obeyed, but I am not willing that your comrades should shed your blood. I order you to march out upon the lake of ice, and I shall leave you there to the mercy of the elements."

    The forty wrestlers were stripped and then, falling into columns of four, marched toward the center of the lake of ice. As they marched they broke into the chant of the arena: "Forty wrestlers, wrestling for Thee, O Christ, to win for Thee the victory and from Thee, the victor's crown!" Through the night Vespasian stood by his campfire and watched. As he waited through the long night, there came to him fainter and fainter the wrestlers' song.

    As morning drew near one figure, overcome by exposure, crept quietly toward the fire; in the extremity of his suffering he had renounced his Lord. Faintly but clearly from the darkness came the song: "Thirty-nine wrestlers, wrestling for Thee, O Christ, to win for Thee the victory and from Thee, the victor's crown!"

    Vespasian looked at the figure drawing close to the fire. Perhaps he saw eternal light shining there toward the center of the lake. Who can say? But off came his helmet and clothing, and he sprang upon the ice, crying, "Forty wrestlers, wrestling for Thee, O Christ, to win for Thee the victory and from Thee, the victor's crown!"

The Concept of a Steward - Additional Food for Thought/Home Study Material

III. THE THIRD WORLD VIEW IS THAT OF A "TOURIST".

A. What is a "TOURIST?"

   1. A Tourist is "an Alien without a purpose." While in the foreign land he has little interest in o loyalty to his homeland from which he is a citizen.

   2. His driving motivation in life is to see and enjoy all the sights and sounds and things that the foreign country in which he is visiting has to offer."

      a. The Tourist will take whatever time is necessary to do it all.
      b. The Tourist will spend whatever money is necessary to have it all.

   3. A Tourist would openly admit to being an Alien if asked, but if carefully watched his lifesty more closely parallels that of a Native.

B. What is a "TOURIST'S" worldview?

   1. The Tourist's life is made up of several, separate and distinct compartments.

      a. a spiritual compartment
      b. a job/business compartment
      c. a social life compartment
      d. a recreational compartment
      e. a life goals compartment
      f. a financial compartment.

   2. The Tourist freely gives God control of the spiritual compartment of his life.

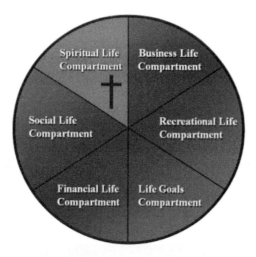

But, the Tourist thinks, "God has left me totally free to do as I please in all the other areas of my life as long as I'm good." In other words, God doesn't really care...

a. . . . how I run my business or do my job as long as I am not an out and out crook or the worst of sluggards.
b. . . .what I watch on TV as long as I don't participate in the sinful activities I watch.
c. . . .how I spend my free time as long as I behave myself.
d. . . .how I spend my money as long as I don't gamble it away. This financial area is where I have focused a major portion of my professional career and ministry efforts.

So, let me take just a minute or two to digress and say a little more about how a Tourist thinks about money.

(1.) A Tourist is happy to acknowledge that God owns everything. But this intellectual acknowledgement has no practical impact on the way he uses his financial resources. He still makes all the decisions about how they will be used.

(2.) The reason that churches and ministries all over America struggles to survive financially is because Tourists spend about 99% of what they make on themselves and their preferred lifestyle.

(3.) In recent research it was revealed that if everyone who claims to be a born-again Christian would just give a tenth of their income, the Kingdom would have access to an additional $133 billion dollars annually. Do you have any idea how much money that is? Or, if you want to use one of the largest ministries in America, it would entirely fund an additional 1,300 Focus on the Family sized ministries annually. Or, we could send an additional 3.3 million missionaries on to the field.

(4.) I personally believe that every dollar that is needed to completely underwrite the needs of every ministry in the world and fulfill the Great Commission in our lifetime is already in the hands of Kingdom citizens. The great tragedy is that the overwhelming majority of it is in the hands of the Tourists who have a totally different mission focus than the King of Kings.

(5.) So, the Tourist reasons God really doesn't care what I do as long as I don't do anything to embarrass Him or His church.

e. Of course, nothing could be further from the truth. But that is how a Tourist, of necessity, must structure his worldview to make any sense out of his Tourist lifestyle.

f. To compare:

The Concept of a Steward - Additional Food for Thought/Home Study Material

(1.) The Alien sings, "I surrender all (and understands those words to mean literally ALL/EVERYTHING)

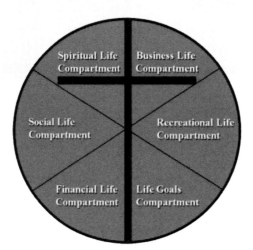

(2.) The Tourist sings, "I surrender all" and understands those words to mean everything in the spiritual compartment in my life (a little of his income, Sunday Mornin attendance, etc.) In other words, he mentally sings, "I surrender all . . .of my spiritual compartment . . ." and he sings it with a totally clear conscience.

g. With this worldview, the Tourist is free to live the vast majority of his life exactly as he pleases with little input or interference from God which allows him to participate and enjoy all the things and activities of this world with no apparent sense of contradictior or feeling of inconsistency.

C. How do these varying worldviews feel about one another?

1. The Native

a. . . . loves and wants the things of the world (because, in his mind, that is all there is in life)

b. . . . hates the Alien (because the Alien is always bent on changing both him and his culture forever). That is exactly what Jesus said would happen to us in John 15:18—19. "If the world (the 'cosmos' – meaning the Natives) hates you, know that it has hated me before it hated you" (esv).

c. . . . tolerates the Tourist (because, even though he is an Alien, he still anxiously and willingly consumes most all of the Natives' goods and services. So it is "good business" to keep him around.)

2. The Tourist

    d. . . . loves and wants the things of the world (because he finds immense pleasure in them).

    e. . . . doesn't really care about the Natives.
        (1.) He is more concerned with the food at the restaurant than the Native waiter or waitress serving it.

        (2.) He is much more interested in the car on the showroom floor than the Native salesman who is selling it.

        (3.) He is more drawn to the videos in the library than the Native librarian who checks them out for him.

        (4.) He is more obsessed with winning the game than for the Natives on the other team who will lose.

        (5.) You see the contrast. The Alien loves people and uses things to benefit them. The Tourist, on the other hand, loves things and uses people to benefit himself.

    f. . . . feels threatened by the Alien (because the Alien stands as a constant reminder of their failure to carry out their assigned mission. And in an attempt to try and justify this failure they often label these Aliens as radicals and holy rollers.)

D. You see the church has slowly and inexorably moved from being a counter-culture in our society to being just one of thousands of sub-cultures that make up our society.

    1. What is a sub-culture? A Sub-Culture is a group of people who want to maintain the distinctives of their group while enjoying the benefits of the larger culture as a whole. They are not at all interested in changing the larger culture. They maintain the attitude that says, "If you don't hassle us about how we are, we won't hassle you about how you are!"

    2. The Chinese people in China Town in San Francisco are not interested in making Denver Chinese. But, likewise, they don't want Denver to force them to use American laundries.

    3. The Polish section of Chicago is not interested in making Indianapolis Polish. But they don't want Indy to insist they stop eating their Polish sausage.

The Concept of a Steward - Additional Food for Thought/Home Study Material

4. But unlike these foreign cultures who brought their distinctives with them, we Christians, have, for the most part, simply modified the world's culture and Christianized it and now claim it is different.

    a. Christian TV networks
    b. Christian book and magazine publishers.
    c. Christian softball leagues
    d. Christian radio stations
    e. Christian Rock and Roll
    f. Christian Psychology
    g. Christian Entertainers
    h. You see, all we have done is merely take the existing worldly culture and its activities and modify them just enough to say they are different from the world wl we leave the bulk of it the same. And if we would be totally honest with ourselves the changes we have made are really more window dressing than reality.

5. What is a counter-culture? It is a group of people whose sole objective is to change existing larger culture and replace it with the distinctives of their own counter-culture.

    a. The teen rebellion of the 60's is a perfect example of a counter-culture. They wer not satisfied with just breaking from traditional culture and having free love, drugs and anti-war sit-ins, they wanted to bring the whole cultural structure down and wanted everyone to adopt their counter-cultural lifestyles and values. And to a ve great extent, they succeeded.

    b. But the best example of an effective counter-culture at work is found right where you might expect to find it; the Handbook for Aliens.

        (1.) Acts 17:2-6 Thessalonica - *"And according to Paul's custom, he went to ther and for three Sabbaths reasoned with them from the Scriptures, explaining and giving evidence that the Christ had to suffer and rise again from the dead, and saying, "This Jesus whom I am proclaiming to you is the Christ." And some of them were persuaded and joined Paul and Silas, along with a great multitude of t. God-fearing Greeks and a number of the leading women. But the Jews, becomin jealous and taking along some wicked men from the market place, formed a mob and set the city in an uproar; and coming upon the house of Jason, they were seeking to bring them out to the people. And when they did not find them, they began dragging Jason and some brethren before the city authorities, shouting, "These men who have upset the world have come here also..." I like the way the King James translates this last verse, "These that have turn the world upside—down are come hither also..."*

(2.) See Paul wasn't coming to Thessalonica to "fit in" with the community and become a respectable citizen of their fair town. He certainly did not come to Thessalonica to see the sights. He was there for one reason and one reason alone; to change that city and culture for Christ. And in following his commission he was "turning the world upside-down!" His counter-cultural revolution was working.

(3.) And may I submit that the exact same counter-cultural revolution initiated by Paul would still work today if we had the courage to employ it.

6. I think the Lord's church has made a terrible error in judgment in recent years.

   a. The error is thinking that the best way to get the world into the church is by trying to make the church as much like the world as we can (of course, we will always keep what we consider to be a safe distance between us) and in making it easier for the world to make the transition many more Natives will join our ranks. The new byword among churches is now "user-friendly" and "seeker sensitive."

   b. The tragedy, unfortunately, is that, as one author has put it. "The church, in trying to lean over and relate to the world, has fallen in."

   c. Now the greatest challenge that lies before us is not getting the world INTO church, it is getting the world OUT OF the church.

   d. Our churches are full of Tourists who profess to be Aliens but who still live the lifestyles of the Natives.

   e. And that, in my humble opinion, is why the church in America which should be shaking this country to its foundations for Christ is, sadly enough, having a relatively minor impact in the life and affairs of America. Our enemies certainly would never accuse us as was Paul of turning the Natives upside-down for Christ.

   f. We are not on this planet to just peacefully coexist with the Natives; we are here to capture the planet for the Commander and Chief of our homeland. We are called to make Aliens out of the Natives!

   g. And to that end and that end alone we have been called.

The Concept of a Steward - Additional Food for Thought/Home Study Material

CONCLUSION:

This world is not a resort, it is a battlefield. It is not our homeland; it is a foreign military outpost. It is not the destination, it is a stopover.

I live in Indiana where the land is flat and much of the state is farming. The two major crops in Indiana are corn and soybeans. And like all good farmers, they periodically rotate their crops. It is interesting that in the year a farmer rotates from growing corn to soybeans inevitably you would see scattered through the soybean filed a few random corn stalks that had grown up from some kernels of corn that didn't get harvested from the previous year's crop.

Many years ago when I was first contemplating these life-changing truths I am sharing with you, my wife and my two oldest daughters, who were maybe seven and five at the time lived in the country and c both sides of our long drive back to our log cabin in the woods were two farm fields, As we were pulling onto our gravel drive one Sunday morning, I looked out at these two soybean fields and for the first tim I really noticed the sporadic corn stalks growing up right in the middle of the soybeans. It was as if God Himself spoke to me at that very moment. I was so overcome by emotion, I stopped the car with my eyes filling with tears and I looke at my wife and daughters and said, "This is what God wants us to be. He wants us to be corn stalk in a soybean field." We may live in a soybean world, but He has called us to stand out, to be differer to be corn stalks for Him – corn stalks in a soybean field!

Many years ago a veteran missionary who had spent 40 years on the mission field was finally coming back to America, the land that he had left nearly a half century earlier. It just so happened that the sh that he was returning on also carried President Teddy Roosevelt from one of his many African huntin expeditions. As the ship arrived in New York Harbor, cheers began to swell as tens of thousands of Americans lined the pier to welcome their President back home. As Roosevelt left the pier so did the crowds and there standing all alone on the pier was the elderly, retiring missionary and there in his hand in one small, tattered bag was all his worldly possessions.

A tear rolled down his old, wrinkled cheek as he muttered to himself sadly, "The President had thousands here to welcome him back home. Not one person is here to welcome me back home." Then that still, small voice that he had come to know and trust for so many years spoke softly and kindly to him, "Ben, it's because your not home yet."

"This world is not my home, I'm just 'a passin' through;
My treasures are laid out somewhere beyond the blue
The angels beckon me from Heaven's open door;
And I can't feel at home in this world any more."

Oh, to long for our homeland like that! Oh, to be so weary from well doing that we yearn for that time of rest in my Fatherland. Oh, to be truly, solely, totally an Alien in this world for Christ – ALL our time, ALL our talents, and ALL our treasures devoted wholly to Him.

would be my greatest desire for each of you that this very moment you would choose to either make a commitment or renew your commitment to being a Resident Alien that is dedicated to the mission that has been set before us – to be corn stalks in a soybean field.

No matter where you stand in your life right now, right this minute you are standing on holy ground. The God of the universe is here this minute seeking those who love Him and those who are willing to deny themselves, (their career preferences, their financial preferences, their retirement preferences, and their lifestyle preferences) and take up their cross and follow Him even to the death to accomplish His mission.

Choose you this day which worldview you will choose, but I hope you will choose to say, "for me and my house, we will be Aliens."

Food for Thought Questions

. What characteristics or lifestyle choices of a Tourist do you most find yourself identifying with?

_____

_____

_____

_____

. How are you trying to fit your relationship with God into the spiritual compartment of your life instead of you trying to fit all the compartments of your life into your relationship with God?

_____

_____

_____

_____

. How might the world be accusing you of "turning the world upside down" (Acts 17:6) for Jesus?

_____

_____

_____

_____

The Focus of a Steward

The One Question that Changes Everything

I like it when someone "cuts to the chase" giving me the bottom line of wha[t] they want to say without including all the details. I am often guilty of helping people finish their sentences so they can more quickly get to the point. I assume some of you might be like that too. So, allow me to boil the quite massive subject of stewardship down to one simple, yet incredibly profound and life-changing question. The question may be simple to ask, it is anythi[ng] but simple to answer.

Before I give you the question, let me first highlight one irrefutable truth that we need to acknowledge[.] This one truth is that God owns everything that exists, including you and me.

Just one of the many passages that confirm God's ownership of everything is found in Job 41:11 wh[ere] God is forcefully questioning Job, "Who has given to Me that I should repay him? Whatever is under [the] whole heaven is Mine." God actually owns us believers in a second way as Paul points out in Titus 2 "Christ Jesus; who gave Himself for us, that He might redeem us from every lawless deed and purify Himself a people for His own possession…." Paul is emphasizing that God is the owner and we are owned. So, when we sit down to prepare a balance sheet of all we own, the list should be very short[. In] fact, the page should be blank. We own nothing, period. It is all His.

Accepting this foundational truth properly prepares us to ask the one question that changes everythi[ng.] Unfortunately, it is not a question we can ask once, answer once and then move on. It is a question [we] must ask routinely, daily, sometimes even hourly. Have I adequately piqued your interest as to what t[his] profound and life-changing stewardship question is?

Here it is - simple to ask, but difficult to answer. "God, what do You want me to do with all that You h[ave] entrusted to me?" We all seem to be more than willing to acknowledge that God owns everything, bu[t] we still seem to continue making all the decisions regarding what we do with what we have. The ultim[ate] objective of our stewardship (management) of God's property is to do with it what He (the Owner) wa[nts] us (the managers) to do with it. What we want to do with our stuff is frankly irrelevant.

Does this idea seem restrictive to you – that you don't get to make any decisions about what will be done with all that you possess? At first blush, it can feel that way. But allow me to put this "you mea[n] I'm not in charge" issue into a broader context.

The Perfect Role Model

Jesus, the one we are all attempting to imitate had no qualms about completely yielding His will to the will of His Father while He was temporarily dwelling on this planet He created. He repeatedly informed people Who was in charge of His life. In John 12:49 He notes the source of all that He says, "For I did not speak on My own initiative, but the Father Himself who sent Me has given Me a commandment as to what to say and what to speak." In John 8:28 He adds all His actions to this, "...I do nothing on My own initiative." In other words, everything that Jesus said and everything that He did was directed by the Father. He was not saying or doing anything apart from His Father's directions.

What about when this God-man and His Father disagreed on a plan of action – for example when Jesus had second thoughts about His pending trip to the cross? Jesus willingly yielded His own will to His Father's. He prayed, "My Father, if it is possible, may this cup be taken from Me. Yet not as I will, but as you will" (Matthew 26:39). God was in charge of every aspect of Jesus' life.

There is an unavoidable question that inevitably emerges from all this. If Jesus willingly yielded all of His words, His actions and even His very life to the will of the Father, dare we be so arrogant or rebellious to make unilateral decisions about our lives and possessions without first consulting with the Father? In other words, are we personally emulating Jesus' submission statement in John 5:30, "I can do nothing on My own initiative...because I do not seek My own will, but the will of Him who sent Me"?

As the game show hosts would always say, "But wait, there's more!" Jesus not only models this for us, He also gives us very direct instruction on how we ought to be handling our Father's property.

As Jesus taught His disciples to pray in His Model Prayer on the Sermon on the Mount, He told them to pray, "Your kingdom come. Your will be done, on earth as it is in heaven" (Matthew 6:10). We have no problem with God's will being done in heaven; the problem is down here on earth, isn't it? The solution to this heaven on earth challenge is for us to willingly allow God's will to rule in how we manage our personal lives and what we do with the temporary possessions we watch over down here. In so doing, each believer will allow God's Kingdom to come and His will to be done in his or her little part of earth as is in heaven.

The Focus of a Steward

Can You Imagine?

Can you imagine what would happen to this world if God's people were to make all their time fully available for His use? What about if they devoted all their talents and whatever was needed of their material resources to carry out God's purposes? What would happen if they cared for their bodies the sacred temple that it really is? What if they saw their employment and careers as an extension God's calling on their lives and a fulfillment of their God-given purpose? What would happen if all t energies were clearly focused on knowing and following their Owner's agenda and being the most obedient and effective managers possible of what He has entrusted to them?

Can you imagine how your personal life would change if each morning as you rose from your bed, you were to genuinely and humbly pray, "Okay, Lord, all that I am and all that I have are at your disposal today. What are your plans for me and my stuff today? Not my will, but Thy will be done t day."

We know those blessed words that we all long to hear from the Lord when we stand before Him, "Well done…" (Matthew 25:21, 23 nasb). I must confess that I have so focused on these two word that until recently I have never really pondered the two adjectives that describe the "slave" who will hear these words. The "well done" commendation goes to the "slave" who is "good and faithful."

He doesn't say, "Well done, efficient and productive slave." He doesn't say, "Well done, doer of great deeds slave." He doesn't say, "Well done, generous and sacrificial slave." He uses two simpl adjectives – good and faithful. As I first considered these words, I rather felt like the bar that Jesus had set in this statement was actually far lower than I had previous understood.

However, as I meditated on these two words further, I began to realize that He may have actually s the bar much higher than I thought. He will someday say well done to his slaves because of what t are (good and faithful) and not because of what they may have done – our being is just as importa as our doing. And for slaves who tend to be more focused on the doing than on the being, this revelation can be quite a sobering realization.

I can think of no better way for us to someday hear, "Well done, good and faithful slave" from our Father than for us to be continually asking Him this one question, "God, what do You want me to c with what You have entrusted to me?" And as He reveals His plans for us and for the stuff He has under our care and management, we need to obediently carry out those plans as faithfully and as well as we can. We need to be good and faithful slaves regardless of how much or how little we h been entrusted with or how much or how little we ultimately accomplish for Him.

I hope you can now see why this one "simple" question, "God, what do You want me to do with w You have entrusted to me," really does change everything. When we faithfully discern and follow Hi directives, we will in a very real and a very tangible way allow God's Kingdom to come and God's v to be done on earth as it is in heaven!

fe Application Questions

What is your initial reaction to this video?

_____

_____

_____

_____

How are you doing with understanding the concept that God owns everything and you own nothing?

_____

_____

_____

_____

How do you feel about the idea that as a steward, you don't get to make any decisions - God gets to make them all?

_____

_____

_____

_____

What areas of your life right now do you think might be most difficult for you to totally surrender to the will of our Father? Why?

_____

_____

_____

_____

The Focus of a Steward

5. Share a story about when you did completely and totally surrender to the Lord's will and what outcome was.

    _____

    _____

    _____

    _____

6. What most amazes you about Jesus' absolute surrender to His Father even to every single wo He spoke?

    _____

    _____

    _____

    _____

7. How hard do you think it was for Jesus to surrender His will to the Father's will, especially wher wanted a different plan than the one God had for Him – to die on Calvary? (Read Matthew 26::

    _____

    _____

    _____

    _____

8. Share a time when you found yourself disagreeing with God about what He wanted you to do a what you wanted to do about a certain situation. How did your conflict get resolved?

    _____

    _____

    _____

    _____

9. How would your life be different if you only spoke words and did things that the Father wanted to speak and do?

    _____

    _____

    _____

    _____

0. As a way of personal assessment, share (be specific) at least one change that you believe you need to make in your life that can help ensure that you will someday hear these blessed words, "Well done, good and faithful slave." (It's okay to be open and honest. We are all a work in progress.)

_____
_____
_____
_____

1. In what ways might you be preventing God's will from reigning here on earth as it now is in Heaven? (Read Matthew 6:10)

_____
_____
_____
_____

2. How do you think asking this one question, "God, what do You want me to do today with what You have entrusted to me?" will change your life if you were to earnestly and sincerely pray it each morning as you awake?

_____
_____
_____
_____

3. Are you afraid to trust God to be totally in charge of your life?

_____
_____
_____
_____

How would your life change if you were to be totally obedient to the will of the Father in how you manage all that He has entrusted to you?

_____
_____
_____
_____

The Focus of a Steward - Additional Food for Thought/Home Study Material

Double Trouble

When we were first married, my wife and I went on a weekend camping trip with my best friend, and his wife at a local lake. We decided to rent canoes for the afternoon. As our leisurely canoe ended, my wife and I rowed up to the dock and stepped out of our canoe. Tom and his wife pull next to our canoe intending to step out of their canoe into our canoe and then on to the dock. To wife got out fine. But when Tom put his first foot into our canoe the shifting of his weight caused canoe to begin drifting away and he found himself in the hilariously untenable position of trying to continue standing in two canoes moving away from each other. Unable to control the drift, he end up doing the splits with hands flailing just before plunging head first into the lake – his feet still hoe over the side of each canoe. We all laughed until we cried at the slap-stick scene before us.

As comical as this scene is to imagine, I think many of us, quite unaware of it, might be in an equ untenable position – trying to straddle two different canoes that are moving in different directions. you have ever been in a canoe, you know that trying to stand up in one canoe can be enough of challenge. Trying to stand up in two canoes, as Tom discovered, is double trouble.

We have two Kingdoms – our spiritual kingdom and our material kingdom. And just as Tom found himself unsuccessfully straddling those two canoes, we too can find ourselves unsuccessfully attempting to straddle our two kingdoms – one foot planted in each even while they continue to c apart – leaving us facing our own double trouble.
The Bible offers several metaphors to expose the untenable position of attempting to live a contradictory double life and the trouble that comes from trying to straddle our two competing "canoes."

James 1:8 tells us that "a double-minded man (is) unstable in all his ways." (Sounds like Tom in th two canoes, doesn't it?) David declares in Psalm 119:113, "I hate the double-minded…" James a in 4:8, "…purify your hearts, you double-minded."

In Psalm 12:2 David provides a different metaphor – that of being double-hearted. In I Timothy 3:8 Paul describes those who are double-tongued. All these phrases describe the contradictory posit of attempting to simultaneously and successfully keep one foot in our spiritual canoe and the othe foot in our material canoe. In doing so, we are facing double trouble.

Jesus said it this way, "No one can serve two masters, for either he will hate the one and love the other, or he will be devoted to the one and despise the other. You cannot serve God and money" (Matthew 6:24). Jesus is expressing the impossibility of trying to successfully straddle these two canoes.

Picture This

Here is how straddling these two canoes can functionally play out in our lives. Our material possessions (time, talents, treasures, toys, etc.) are in our material canoe. And on occasion, we are asked, compelled, coerced or convicted to give some of our stuff from our material canoe to our spiritual canoe, to be used for spiritual purposes. When we transfer some of our material assets over to the spiritual canoe, it is recorded, reported and/or recognized.

Contrast this picture with an alternative picture. We wholly and solely live in only one canoe – our spiritual canoe. At our conversion we willingly transferred everything we were and everything we had – and I mean everything – from our material canoe to our spiritual canoe and we abandoned our material canoe. We sang "All to Jesus I surrender, all to Him I freely give." And really meant all – everything we have and everything we are is His. We were all in the spiritual canoe. (Not that any of our material stuff was ever really ours in the first place, but we did finally acknowledge that we had wrongly confiscated it and we were now willingly returning it to the rightful Owner.) [See Psalms 24:1; 50:10-12.]

From that day forward it has no longer been a question of what will we transfer from our material canoe to our spiritual canoe. Everything we possess and everything we ever will possess is already in our spiritual canoe to be used for Kingdom purposes whenever and however it is needed by our sovereign King. Let me ask you to think back. Did you indeed surrender and transfer all the possessions in your material canoe now and forever into your spiritual canoe when you surrendered to Christ? Did you really "surrender all?"

If the answer is yes, then your giving decisions are not really giving decisions. They could more accurately be described as deployment decisions. The term giving carries with it the implication that we are taking something from our material canoe and "giving" it to our spiritual canoe to be used for spiritual purposes. The term deployment, to the contrary, simply focuses on how these resources already in the spiritual canoe will be utilized to produce maximum impact and benefit for the King to whom these assets already belong.

If we attempt to live with one foot in our spiritual canoe and the other one in our material canoe, we will find ourselves, double-minded, double-hearted, double-tongued and with a severe case of double-vision. We will indeed find ourselves continually living with double trouble.

The Focus of a Steward - Additional Food for Thought/Home Study Material

Vision Test

It is interesting to note that right after Jesus tells us that we should not lay up treasures for ourselves in our material canoe, but we should instead lay up treasures in our spiritual canoe, and right before He tells us that we cannot simultaneously live in two different canoes (God and riches), He adds a powerful illustration in Matthew 6:22-23, "The eye is the lamp of the body. So, if your eye is healthy, your whole body will be full of light, but if your eye is bad, your whole body will be full of darkness. If then the light in you is darkness, how great is the darkness!"

It is impossible for our two eyes to simultaneously focus on two different images. Have you ever intentionally crossed your eyes? If you have you know that when you point your eyes in different directions, you can't see anything clearly with either eye. We cannot focus on both our spiritual and our material canoes at the same time and if we do we will find, like my friend Tom, that we are in compromising position that can never be maintained nor can it ever be totally fulfilling.

Where are You Standing?

Ask yourself, "Where am I standing right now? Am I trying to straddle these two different canoes, hoping to enjoy the best that both canoes have to offer?" If the answer is, "Yes," then you are indeed in double trouble. May I suggest that the superior option for us, if we have not already done so, is to transfer everything we have into one canoe – our spiritual canoe. In doing so, something glorious will happen. We will find ourselves becoming singled-minded, single-hearted, single-tongued and single-visioned. We will now be single-focused on what God wants us to do with what we are carrying of His material things in His spiritual canoe to be used for His divine purposes for His ultimate glory. If we get into the right canoe, the spiritual canoe, heading in the right direction with an eternal perspective in mind, we will experience what Paul describes in I Timothy 6:19 as "life indeed." Let's think: Double trouble or life indeed? Not really a very difficult choice, is it? Let me encourage you, starting today, be all in your spiritual canoe!

Food for Thought Questions

1. In what ways do you find yourself trying to live a *two-canoe* life?

_____

_____

_____

_____

2. Do you have trouble staying single-minded, single-hearted, single-tongued and single-visioned in your daily walk with the Lord? How often are you tempted to climb back into your material canoe?

_____

_____

_____

_____

3. What is it going to take for you to put all your material "stuff" into your spiritual canoe and keep it there?

_____

_____

_____

_____

The Characteristics of a Steward

The Defining Characteristics of a Good and Faithful Steward

Tragic as it is, the concept of stewardship is so poorly taught and so poorly practiced among followers of Jesus that it is necessary to provide a clear description of how a good and faithful steward should live. The life of an obedient steward possesses three dominant life-characteristics. As we consider each of these characteristics, may it enable us to better assess how well we are personally living the life of a good and faithful steward.

A Good and Faithful Steward Lives an Examined Life

This practice of living a life of regular self-examination is often referenced in the Bible. In II Corinthians 13:5 Paul told the believers in Corinth, "Examine yourselves to see whether you are in the faith; test yourselves…" He also tells them in I Corinthians 11:28 that, "A man ought to examine himself before he eats of the bread and drinks of the cup (communion)." Even Jeremiah exhorts his people Lamentations 3:40, "Let us test and examine our ways."

There is nothing more appropriate for a faithful manager of someone else's resources than to routinely examine how effectively he is carrying out his responsibilities. A steward will continually examine his behavior, his motives, his thoughts, his attitudes, the direction of his life and how well he is imitating life of Jesus.

Unfortunately, we often only examine our lives when something is going wrong or we face some significant crisis. In the midst of that trial, we finally pause to take stock of our lives to determine what might have caused this difficult situation. Crisis examination is certainly better than no examination at all, but may I suggest that a good and faithful steward will be doing routine self-examination as part his daily life.

I have been told by more than one pilot that a plane when in the air is off course about 95% of the time due to wind currents, barometric pressure, etc. Because of this, the pilot must be vigilant in making continual minor course corrections to bring the plane back on course. If he does not, he will find, after several hours of flying that his plane is actually hundreds of miles off course.

The good and faithful steward is like the attentive pilot in flight – continually examining the course of his or her life to determine if it is still following the flight pattern that has been set by the "Tower." The steward will routinely make whatever midcourse corrections to his life that are needed regardless of how subtle or how dramatic they need to be. He recognizes that the gravitational pull of this world and the unpredictable winds of temptation can very quickly get him off course.

Socrates correctly concluded, "The unexamined life is not worth living."

So, would the word examined describe your life?

Good and Faithful Steward Lives a Controlled Life

Living a controlled life is a foundational characteristic of a good and faithful steward. Self-control is one of the fruits of the Spirit (Galatians 5:23). Paul repeats several times in his letter to Titus that believers are to live a controlled life. Elders are to have their lives under control (Titus 1:8). Older men are to be self-controlled (Titus 2:2). Young men and women are to be self-controlled as well (Titus 2:5-6).

Paul uses the discipline and self-control of an athlete in training to illustrate the controlled life of a steward (1 Corinthians 9:25). Just two verses later he applies self-control to himself when he says, "But I discipline my body and keep it under control…"

I think Solomon makes this point best when he says in Proverbs 25:28, "A man without self-control is like a city broken into and left without walls." There is nothing to contain him and he lives a life that is out of control in one or more ways.

We all know people who lack self-control. They cannot control their tempers. They cannot control their appetites. They cannot control their emotions. They cannot control their tongues. They cannot control their sex drives. They cannot control their spending. In one or more ways they are lacking self-control. They are "like a city broken into and left without walls."

The good and faithful steward, to the contrary, is constantly restraining and retraining his natural impulses to keep all of these fleshly desires (both good and bad) under control. He is diligently working day-by-day and often minute-by-minute to keep his head in the game and not allow "the desires of the flesh and the desires of the eyes and pride in possessions…" (I John 2:16) to break down the walls of self-control that is a defining characteristic of a good and faithful steward.

John Milton said well, "He who reins within himself and rules passions, desires and fears is more than a king." The steward who is in control will be both useful and effective in obediently serving his Master. So, would the word controlled describe your life?

The Characteristics of a Steward

A Good and Faithful Steward Lives a Sacrificial Life

The third characteristic that will always be commonly seen in the life of a good and faithful steward sacrifice. We simply cannot be good and faithful stewards if sacrifice is not a part of our lives.

Paul calls us to be "living sacrifices" (Romans 12:1). Jesus challenges every steward that if he wants to follow Him, "let him deny himself and take up his cross daily and follow me" (Luke 9:23). The cross in Jesus' day was used for only one purpose, to kill someone. So the imagery He is giving us is quite dramatic. He is not calling us to a one-time sacrificial death for "the cause." The sacrifice He is describing here is to be a daily sacrifice. Each day, we are to put to death our wishes, our desires, agenda, our comforts, our free time and our hopes for the greater good of the Kingdom and the wo we seek to win.

In his book The Kingdom and the Cross, James Bryan Smith suggests that, "If our God is self-sacrificing and seeks to bless others who have done nothing to merit it, then we should be people are self-sacrificing and who bless others who have not earned it."

There is no more powerful demonstration of a good and faithful steward than when he willingly and sacrificially gives to others without any consideration of their worthiness to receive his gift.

Regardless of how great or small the need or opportunity, he gladly sacrifices whatever he currently manages for the good of others.

John gives us the ultimate extent to which we must be willing to live a sacrificial life. He said in I John 3:16, "By this we know love, that He laid down His life for us, and we ought to lay down our lives for the brothers."

If sacrificing our lives is the maximum sacrifice we might be called to make as a steward, it seems to put into a clear context the modest sacrifices we make when we give some of the money, or the time or the talents we have been given to manage to help others.
So, would the word sacrificial describe your life?

If we want to be identified as a good and faithful steward and someday hear those wonderful words "Well done," we must (1) routinely examine ourselves to be sure that our lives are on the right course that has been set by our Master. (2) We need to be vigilant that we control our appetites and impulse to ensure that they do not end up controlling us. (3) We need to be regularly and generously sacrific what we have been entrusted with in hopes of bringing a little bit of heaven to those who are here on earth. Living the life of a good and faithful steward is a tremendous challenge. Are you up to the challenge?

Life Application Questions

. What is your initial reaction to this video?

_____

_____

_____

_____

. Which of these three areas of life stewardship (the examined life, the controlled life, or the sacrificial life) do you personally most struggle with? Why?

_____

_____

_____

_____

3. When do you most often find yourself willing and desiring to carefully examine your life? Are you more of a routine self-examination person or a life-crisis examination person?

_____

_____

_____

_____

4. Why do we so seldom take the time to do a thorough self-assessment of our lives and the direction we are headed?

_____

_____

_____

_____

The Characteristics of a Steward

5.   Share some examples of people you know who are living examples of what Proverbs 25:28 say
     "A man without self-control is like a city broken into and left without walls."

     _____
     _____
     _____
     _____

6.   In what areas of your life do you currently struggle most to keep under control? (We all have the
     so you are not alone.)

     _____
     _____
     _____
     _____

7.   What do you think Paul means when he says in Romans 12:1 that we are to be "living sacrifices

     _____
     _____
     _____
     _____

8.   How does the ownership issue of our possessions hinder us from living a more sacrificial and
     generous life than we do now?

     _____
     _____
     _____
     _____

What would be the hardest material thing for you to let go of (sacrifice), if the Lord were to call you to release it?

_____

_____

_____

_____

). For you, what is most challenging about John's statement in I John 3:16, "By this we know love, that He laid down His life for us, and we ought to lay down our lives for the brothers"?

_____

_____

_____

_____

1. How do you react to what James Bryan Smith wrote, "If our God is self-sacrificing and seeks to bless others who have done nothing to merit it, then we should be people who are self-sacrificing and who bless others who have not earned it?" If we really believed this statement and really applied it to our daily lives, how might this change how we actually give to others?

_____

_____

_____

_____

2. Share with the group what has been the most sacrificial gift you have ever made in your life?

_____

_____

_____

_____

Examining Our Purpose

Are You Living Your Life on Purpose or by Accident?

People have often asked me what I mean when I encourage people to pla[n] their lives on purpose. My answer is simple. You can choose to live your lif[e] one of two ways: you can either live your life on purpose, or you can live yo[ur] life by accident. In other words, you can plan your life and live your plan, o[r] you can simply let the flow of life events and circumstances sweep you do[wn] the river of time taking you wherever it will. The latter, sadly, is the way mos[t] people live their lives—by accident. The former is how God created us to live—on purpose. (You can see this in passages like Ephesians 5:15-16 and Psalm 90:12.)

Some might claim that there is something unspiritual about making plans, but for those of us who d[o] we are in good company. God made plans. (See Hebrews 11:40a, Jeremiah 29:11, Ephesians 1:1[1].) Paul made plans. (See 2 Corinthians 1:15-17, Romans 15:24.) And we are encouraged to make pl[ans] (See Proverbs 16:3, 20:18, 21:5.)

Unfortunately, when it comes to building one's financial "empire" we can often find ourselves doing it without any real divine purpose behind it. Successful people continue to build up their "pile of stuff" because they have become exceedingly good at what they do. They also find great emotiona[l] enjoyment and personal satisfaction in building, so they keep on building without ever giving much thought to where it will end up.

However, I think there is a foundational question that we, as believers, need to ask ourselves, "Wha[t] is my purpose for continuing to build my financial empire when my pile of stuff is already higher than[I] will ever need it to be?" Jesus tells us plainly that accumulating excess material possessions as a so[me] end in itself is entirely futile. Jesus states, "For what will it profit a man if he gains the whole world an[d] forfeits his soul?" (Matthew 16:26). For those who do this are like the rich farmer who planned to tea[r] down his smaller barns and build bigger barns to hold his surplus wealth. Remember, Jesus called [him] a fool.

There is no greater example of the utter folly of building without a purpose than the story of Sarah Winchester. Sarah was the wife of William Winchester, the only son of Oliver Winchester, the founde[r] and owner of the Winchester Repeating Arms Company. Sarah and William had a daughter who die[d] shortly after birth in 1866. This was followed by the death of her father-in-law (in 1880) and then her husband just a few months later (in 1881), leaving her with a fifty percent ownership in the company and an income of $1,000 a day (about $21,000 a day in current dollars).

Sarah believed that her family was under some kind of a curse and consulted a medium to determin[e] what she should do. The medium told her that her family was indeed cursed by the spirits of all the people that the Winchester rifle had killed. She should move out west and build a house for herself and all the tormented spirits who suffered because of her family. The medium also told her that if construction on this house were to ever cease, she would immediately die.

In 1884 Sarah moved to California and began one of the most bizarre building stories in American history. She began spending her $20 million inheritance and regular income to buy and begin renovating an eight-room farmhouse in what is now San Jose, California. From that day forward construction continued nonstop, twenty-four hours a day, seven days a week until Sarah's death at age eighty-three—a total of thirty-eight years. She kept no less than twenty-two carpenters busy continuously. The sounds of hammers and saws could be heard throughout the day and night for almost four decades.

At its zenith, this seven story house contained 160 rooms, forty bedrooms, forty-seven fireplaces, seventeen chimneys, and 10,000 windowpanes. What made Sarah's lifetime building project so bizarre was that it had no discernable architectural purpose or plan behind it. Closet doors opened to solid walls. Windows were in the floor. Stairways led to nowhere. Railings were installed upside down. Drawers were only one inch deep. Trapdoors were everywhere. Blind chimneys stopped short of the ceiling. There were double-back hallways. Doors opened to steep drops to the lawn below. Many of the bathrooms had glass doors. The list of oddities runs into the dozens. Could there be a more classic example of the ultimate outcome of "building without a purpose?"

We may think that what we are building is not bizarre like Sarah Winchester's construction project. Let me suggest that unless there is a divine purpose behind why we are doing, God may actually find it as meaningless and bizarre as the Sarah Winchester Mystery House. Paul addresses this very issue in 1 Corinthians 3:12-15 when he says,

Now if any man builds on the foundation with gold, silver, precious stones, wood, hay, straw, each man's work will become evident; for the day will show it because it is to be revealed with fire, and the fire itself will test the quality of each man's work. If any man's work which he has built on it remains, he will receive a reward. If any man's work is burned up, he will suffer loss; but he himself will be saved, yet so as through fire.

May I ask, "What foundation are you building on? What materials are you building with? And why are you building what you are building?"

I think John Wesley had it right when he said, "Gain all you can. Save all you can. Give all you can." If we adhere to this compelling "financial triad" as we labor on our building projects, we will be building on a solid foundation utilizing building materials of heavenly "gold, silver, and precious stones." And in our building efforts we will discover that we are indeed living life on purpose.

Examining Our Purpose

Life Application Questions

1. What is your initial reaction to this video?

    _____

    _____

    _____

    _____

2. Do you think it is a lack of faith to make plans for the future?
    a. Read about purpose: Ephesians 5:15-16, Psalm 90:12
    b. Read about God making plans: Hebrews 11:40a, Jeremiah 29:11, Ephesians 1:11
    c. Read about Paul making plans: 2 Corinthians 1:15-17, Romans 15:24
    d. Read about people making plans: Proverbs 16:3, 20:18, 21:5

    _____

    _____

    _____

    _____

3. In what ways do you think it might be wrong to make plans for the future? Read James 4:13-
    and compare the above verses with this passage. Why is making plans considered right in so
    places and then wrong in others?

    _____

    _____

    _____

    _____

4. Do you consider yourself rich? Who are you comparing yourself to? Why must we be very car
    about failing to recognize just how rich we are? Will knowing your income compared to the res
    of the world's income change your current lifestyle, attitudes and/or behavior? If so, how? If n
    why not?

    _____

    _____

    _____

    _____

5. Read I Corinthians 3:12-15 and discuss what kinds of materials might be categorized as the
    "heavenly materials" that we should be building with?

    _____

    _____

    _____

    _____

6. What do you think of John Wesley's statement "Gain all you can, save all you can, give all you can"? How might this way of thinking change the way you are currently working, handling money and giving?

_____

_____

_____

_____

7. What is your assessment of what Sarah Winchester spent her life and her vast fortune to build? (Should we take into consideration the fact that it was all built of the highest quality materials by hundreds of highly skilled craftsmen?)

_____

_____

_____

_____

8. What do you understand your unique God-given purpose to be? Why has God put you on this planet – at just this time in history and in just this place – America (and not the slums of Calcutta or the rural bush in Africa)? What are you here for?

_____

_____

_____

_____

9. How is what you are currently doing with your time, your talents and your treasures helping you to fulfill your unique life-purpose?

_____

_____

_____

_____

10. If you continue on the course your life is headed now, will you be happy with what you have spent your life "building"?

_____

_____

_____

_____

Examining Our Purpose - Additional Food for Thought/Home Study Material

Discovering Your Fire Within[1]

The overwhelming majority of people on this planet never really discover the unique life purpose for which God created them. It seems that the materialism and the pursuit of all things good in this life have overshadowed the deeper meaning of our life's purpose. Few people, even serious Christians, are tuned in to the idea of finding and fulfilling their life purpose and divine destiny.

I think this is the reason Rick Warren's The Purpose-Driven Life was such a runaway best seller even in secular circles. His book touched a nerve in all of us who want to believe that life in general—and individual lives specifically—must have some greater meaning and purpose. Oliver Wendell Holmes described the sad futility most people experience when he wrote, "Many people die with their music still in them." In other words, what all these people could have been, and should have been, was never realized.

In the story of Esther, during a secret meeting, her Uncle Mordecai reveals to her a plot to kill all the Jews (of which she is one). What he said to her was hugely profound. He connected this crisis of extinction for the Jews to her unlikely rise to become Queen of Persia. Mordecai asks her, "And who knows whether you have not attained royalty for such a time as this?" (Esther 4:14). He was basically saying, "Could it be, Esther, that the reason God made you Queen is because He wants you to save His people from destruction?" Talk about feeling a sense of destiny.

There is something deep within our very beings that nags at us to find some meaning and purpose for our lives. Too often, we try to satisfy this nagging need for purpose by making lots of money, accumulating lots of nice things, being a workaholic, pursuing power and prestige, etc. A multimillionaire told me some years ago—after spending a lifetime dedicated to climbing the ladder of success—that once he had finally reached the top he discovered, to his bitter disappointment, that "the ladder was leaning against the wrong wall." All that he had gained in the climb to "success" was totally overshadowed by what he had lost in its pursuit—his health, his wife, his family, and his friendships.

So, how can we discover what God has really created us to do? There are three areas that must be considered if we are going to find our life purpose.

> #1. God has hard-wired into each of us certain God-given passions. These God-given passions are the things that excite us, motivate us, and bring us enjoyment. It may be sports, building things, some moral or social cause, learning, or the arts. Each of us possesses a unique combination of God-given passions. God gave us those passions to point us towards a specific purpose and enable us to fulfill it.

> #2. God has given us a unique set of talents. These God-given talents are the things that come naturally to us. For some, it is the ability to sing or teach or an athletic ability or some mechanical insight or understanding. Some people are incredibly artistic, while

1 Excepted from E. G. "Jay" Link, Spiritual Thoughts on Material Things: Thirty Days of Food for Thought (Xulon Press, Longwood, FL, 2009), pp. 125-128.

others have a natural ability to dream of what could be. The way to know you have a God-given talent is that you are better at it than you should be for the time and effort you have put into it. The youth who picks up a basketball and right from the first time he touches the ball he is above average at the game. Or the young lady who captivates all by her singing and yet has never once taken a voice lesson. I had a friend in college who had never taken one piano lesson yet he could sit down and play the piano

like he had been taking lessons all his life. He could not read a note of music, but if he could hear the music, he could play it. God has given each of us a unique set of God-given talents for a purpose.

#3. God has planted within each of our hearts some God-given purpose. This God-given purpose has some divine, eternal intention for which we have been created. I am not talking about a general purpose like worshiping Him or living a godly life. These things apply to all of us. I am talking about some specific purpose that He wants us to accomplish for Him with our lives.

When you find something to do with your life that is fueled by your God-given passions, utilizes your God-given talents, and accomplishes a God-given purpose, you will find what I call "the fire within." Engaging in this activity will bring complete fulfillment and will leave you totally energized. It is like when you hit the sweet spot on a baseball bat—you hit a homerun! Now do not think that in order to find your fire within, you need to go into some fulltime Christian work, become a pastor, missionary, or Bible college professor. Obviously, those are worthy life purposes for those whom God has given the passion, talent, and calling to do those specific kinds of ministries.

Instead, you may be like one Christian man I know. Since he was sixteen years old, he felt called by God to be a businessman. He used his passions and talents coupled with this God-given call to build a very substantial family business. He and his family are now impacting people worldwide with their Christian witness. They also have millions of dollars to give away from the success God has given them. I know another commercial real estate developer who is using his passion for real estate and his talent for making multi-million dollar deals so he can support Kingdom causes that God has laid on his heart. This is his God-given purpose.

Most of you have seen how Tony Dungy, retired coach for the Indianapolis Colts, has used his God-given passion and talent for football as a platform to share the message of Christ with literally millions of people all over the world who would otherwise never step foot into a church building—another worthy God-given purpose.

Examining Our Purpose - Additional Food for Thought/Home Study Material

If you do not want to die with "your music still in you," then I encourage you to discover what God created you for by identifying your God-given passions, your God-given talents, and your God-given purpose. Find something you love and are gifted to do that will fulfill a calling and have an eternal impact. In so doing, you will indeed discover your fire within.

Food for Thought Questions

1. What are the things in your life that you are most passionate about?

_____

_____

_____

_____

2. If you were to ask other people what your greatest gifts are, what do you think they would you? Ask them.

_____

_____

_____

_____

3. How can you use your God-given passions and God-given talents to achieve some specific divine purpose?

_____

_____

_____

_____

• 49

Examining Our Worth

How Do You Calculate How Much You Are Worth?

Often this question is answered with another question, "That depends, who wants to know?" If the Internal Revenue Service is asking, we attempt to make everything appear to be worth as little as possible. We will apply min and lack of marketability discounts, utilize low appraisals, apply book value etc. – attempting to minimize our worth. If, on the other hand, it is our ban who is asking, we amazingly become worth considerably more as we atter to paint the most optimistic, best-case-scenario picture to our lender.

May I suggest, however, that as believers, we need to answer this question in a different way. If we want to most accurately calculate how much we are really worth, we need to utilize three entirely different types of "valuation methods."

Valuation Method #1

We Need to Value Our Life Worth Rather Than Our Net Worth

Many years ago an older, wealthy gentleman shared his story with me. His singular goal in life was to become a millionaire. He imagined this task like climbing a sheer cliff wall. One hand of rock after another, slowly, inch by inch he climbed it. He said, "After spending virtually my entire adult life struggling to get to the top, I was at last able to reach up and grab the top of the cliff. Then slowly I was able to pull myself up to finally, after all these years, see what was there. And do you know what I saw when I pulled myself up," he asked? "Nothing. There was absolutely nothing there." How tragically sad.

The last thing we should want to do is spend our lives climbing the ladder of success only to realize once we finally do reach the top that our ladder is leaning against the wrong wall. And all that we rea wanted in life we do not have and all we do have is not what we really want.

Jesus told us, "…a man's life does not consist in the abundance of his possessions" (Luke 12:15, n He adds in the parable of the sower, "…the deceitfulness of riches and the desires for other things enter in and choke the word…" (Mark 4:19, nasb). If you are valuing your net worth more than your worth, you are indeed climbing up the wrong ladder.
So what is your life worth? Paul reminds us, "But God demonstrates His own love toward us, in that while we were yet sinners, Christ died for us" (Romans 5:8, nasb). John adds, "See how great a love the Father has bestowed on us, that we would be called children of God; and such we are" (I John 3:1, nasb). This glorious truth makes us exceedingly valuable.

Some years ago a good friend and client of mine, John Bandimere, invited me to attend his big national drag race event. He gave me a pass that let me go up to his personal tower suite with air conditioned comfort, eat all the free food I wanted, and sit in the best seats at the track. I got to go right down on the track's starting line and he even took me into the pit area. It was an incredible thrill I felt so important that day. I wanted to tell everyone as I walked around with my VIP pass hanging around my neck, "I personally know the owner of this place!" As I was basking in the thrill of my VIP status, it occurred to me this is exactly the same attitude we ought to have as we travel through life

...alking around proudly saying, "I personally know the Owner of this place and that makes me somebody ...ortant!"

...r real worth in this life will never be found in the stuff we collect; it will be found in the fact that we ...sonally know the Owner!

...ng Valuation Method #1, what are you really worth?

...uation Method #2

...Need to Value Our Internal Acquisitions Rather Than Our External Acquisitions

...ul addresses just how important it is to be pursuing internal, spiritual acquisitions and not material, ...ernal ones. He says, "But those who desire to be rich fall into temptation, into a snare, into many ...nseless and harmful desires that plunge people into ruin and destruction. For the love of money is a root ...all kinds of evils. It is through this craving that some have wandered away from the faith and pierced ...mselves with many pangs. But as for you, O man of God, flee these things [external acquisitions]. Pursue ...nteousness, godliness, faith, love, steadfastness, gentleness" [internal acquisitions] (I Timothy 6:9-11, esv).

...ul goes on to specifically encourage women to focus on internal, spiritual acquisitions and not external, ...aterial ones when he instructs them, "Your adornment should be not an exterior one, consisting of braided ...r or gold jewelry or fine clothing, but the interior disposition of the heart, consisting in the imperishable ...ality of a gentle and peaceful spirit, so precious in the sight of God" (I Peter 3:3-4, NJB). How diligently are ...u seeking to internally acquire the mind and nature of Christ? This is what Paul says is "precious [valuable] ...the sight of God."

...ere is no more poignant expression of the folly of valuing what we are worth by our external, material ...quisitions instead of by our internal, spiritual ones than when Jesus confronts the Laodiceans in Revelation ...17. He exposes them saying, "For you say, 'I am rich, I have prospered, and I need nothing' [external ...quisitions], not realizing that you are wretched, pitiable, poor, blind, and naked" [internal acquisitions] (esv). ...e Laodiceans were valuing the wrong balance sheet.

...henever I read this passage, I cannot help but remember the fairy tale, The Emperor's New Clothes. Two ...nmen convince the Emperor that the material they are making his new clothes with is so fine that idiots ...d fools are unable to even see it. The Emperor, in order to avoid being labeled an idiot or a fool, convinces ...mself that he can see the new clothes and proudly parades down the streets of the city in his underwear ...lieving that he was clothed in the finest garments, when in reality he was clothed in nothing at all. The very ...ng he was trying to avoid is the very thing he ended up proving – he, like the Laodiceans, was indeed a ...ol and an idiot.

...his is what will happen to us, if we choose to calculate what we are worth based upon our external ...quisitions instead of our internal ones. We must understand this, "What the world esteems greatly [external ...quisitions], God disregards and what God esteems greatly [internal acquisitions], the world disregards."

...sing Valuation Method #2, what are you really worth?

Examining Our Worth

Valuation Method #3

We Need to Value Our Eternal Assets Rather Than Our Temporal Assets

The Bible is very clear that our temporal assets will do us no good after we leave this planet. Solomon tells us (and he ought to know), "Wealth is worthless in the day of wrath [temporal assets], but righteousness [eternal assets] delivers from death" (Proverbs 11:4, niv).

Jesus reminds us that even a temporal balance sheet that would include everything on earth is still wholly worthless on the judgment day. He tells us, "For what does it profit a man to gain the whole world [temporal assets], and forfeit his soul [eternal assets]?" (Mark 8:36, nasb)

You may recall in Daniel where God writes on the wall an unreadable message to King Belshazzar. He calls for Daniel to interpret God's message. Daniel translates, "You praised the gods of silver and gold, of bronze, iron, wood and stone… [temporal assets]. But you did not honor the God who holds in his hand your life and all your ways…You have been weighed on the scales and found wanting [eternal assets]" (Daniel 5:23b, 27, niv). We must be ever mindful that on God's eternal scales, our accumulated, temporal assets, no matter how great they might be, weigh nothing.

Because of this, Jesus commands us, "Do not lay up for yourselves treasures upon earth… [temporal assets], but lay up for yourselves treasures in heaven…" [eternal assets] (Matthew 6:19-20, nasb).

Receiving rewards (treasures) in heaven is not taught in most churches. But the Bible is very clear that even though our salvation cannot be earned by any good works, our "rewards in heaven" will be directly tied to our good works. Twenty-nine times the Greek word for rewards is used in the New Testament. Here are some of the ways the New Testament tells us to grow our eternal assets (rewards/treasures) in heaven: accepting persecution (Matthew 5:10-12), loving our enemies (Luke 6:35), giving generously (Matthew 6:2-4), praying (Matthew 6:6), fasting (Matthew 6:18), showing hospitality (Matthew 10:41), showing kindness towards others (Mark 9:41), doing good deeds (I Corinthians 3:10, Colossians 3:24), and sharing our faith (I Corinthians 3:8, I Corinthians 9:17-18).

When we calculate what we are worth, are we looking at what we have here and now or what we will have then and there? What we keep now, we will lose forever and what we lose now, we will keep forever.

How much would you be worth if you were to eternally relocate today? This question ought to give of us cause to pause and reflect.

Using Valuation Method #3, what are you really worth?

If we want to know how much we are really worth, we cannot use the world's valuation methods because they are inaccurate and misleading and will only provide us with a distorted sense of worth. God's valuation methods, on the other hand, are true and accurate and by utilizing them as our standard measure of worth, we can be sure that in God's economy, we can be indeed rich in both this life and the next, regardless of what our current balance sheet may show.

fe Application Questions

What is your initial reaction to this video?

_____

_____

_____

_____

Why are these different valuation methods so important for us to understand and utilize particularly in our highly affluent society?

_____

_____

_____

_____

In what ways might you relate to the businessman who spent his life climbing the sheer cliff to get rich only to discover once he got to the top, there was nothing there?

_____

_____

_____

_____

Why is it so easy to find ourselves climbing the ladder of success often completely unaware that this ladder is leaning against the wrong wall and what we really want in life, we will not have and what we do have, we do not really want?

_____

_____

_____

_____

What is your reaction to the statement, "Our real worth in this life will never be found in the stuff we collect; it will be found in the fact that we personally know the Owner"?

_____

_____

_____

_____

• 5 3

Examining Our Worth

6. List what the internal assets are that we possess and then answer why these should be of greater value to us than the external material assets in our life.

    _____

    _____

    _____

    _____

7. Revelation 3:17 says, "For you say, 'I am rich, I have prospered, and I need nothing' [external acquisitions], not realizing that you are wretched, pitiable, poor, blind, and naked" [internal acquisitions] (esv). In what ways might we Christians in America be guilty of this same false valuation method?

    _____

    _____

    _____

    _____

8. Would you agree or disagree with the statement, "What the world esteems greatly [external acquisitions], God disregards and what God esteems greatly [internal acquisitions], the world disregards." Why or why not?

    _____

    _____

    _____

    _____

9. In what ways will we be receiving eternal rewards for our life of faithful stewardship? Should we be investing in this life in ways that will make us richer in the next one? How can we do that?

    _____

    _____

    _____

    _____

0. The video said, "When we calculate what we are worth, are we looking at what we have here and now or what we will have then and there? What can we do as believers to stay more focused on the then and there and not on the here and now in regards to the value of what we have?

_____

_____

_____

_____

1. Based upon these three new valuation methods to determine your worth, how do they change your perspective on how well off you are?

_____

_____

_____

_____

Examining Our Possessions

Do You Love the World?

The Bible is full of caution lights warning us when we are about to head off course and into spiritual trouble. John issues one of those warnings to us, not love the world or anything in the world. If anyone loves the world, the lo the Father is not in him" (1 John 2:15).

It is quite interesting that John tells us to not love (agape) the world (cosmo with the very same Greek words that Jesus used when He told us that "Go so loved (agape) the world (cosmos)…" (John 3:16). So, since we know that God cannot contradic Himself, there must be a way in which we are to love the world and a way in which we are to not lo the world. We can understand this apparent contradiction in the following way.

A spiritually healthy love for the world desires to give something to it [the gospel]. The rest of John 3 says, "For God so loved the world that he gave."

A spiritually sick love for the world desires to get something from it I John 2:16 says, "For everything the world—the cravings of sinful man, the lust of his eyes and the boasting of what he has and doe comes not from the Father but from the world."

What is troubling about John's warning is that it doesn't give us much guidance on how to identify whether we do in fact love the world and the things of the world. Is it enough that we say we love C and we don't love the world or the things of the world? Is our profession enough? I don't know ab you, but my words have often betrayed me. I have found on occasion that I am not really what I say am. (What is on the outside is not what is on the inside.) So, it is necessary for us to look deeper tha just our words. We must look at our hearts and observe our actions to determine if we are indeed i love with the world and the things of the world.

I have identified four, flashing, "caution lights" that should warn us that we might indeed have gotter an illicit love affair with the world and the things of this world.

Caution Light #1

We are falling in love with the world…when we are never quite satisfied with what we have

Solomon says in Ecclesiastes 5:10, "Whoever loves money never has money enough; whoever love wealth is never satisfied with his income." Are you truly satisfied with what you have right now? If yc never got anything more for the rest of your life would that be ok with you?

Or, do you find yourself drawn to the newest technology gadget, a bigger or better car, another exot travel destination, the latest fashion, a newer or bigger home, or another way to make more money. your life characterized by wanting and getting more stuff?

Solomon again warns us in Ecclesiastes 6:7, "All man's efforts are for his mouth, yet his appetite is never satisfied." Is your appetite satisfied with what you have right now or will it take more?

If "more" is descriptive of the way you think about the things of the world and the way you live in the world, Caution Light #1 is flashing and you may indeed be involved in an illicit love affair with the world that can destroy your pure and holy relationship to your bride groom, Jesus.

Caution Light #2

We are falling in love with the world…when the things we own end up owning us.

Jesus reminded us that we only have one throne and He wants to be on it. He tells us in Matthew 6:24, "No one can serve two masters; for either he will hate the one and love the other, or he will be devoted to one and despise the other. You cannot serve God and wealth."

Demas was one of Paul's mission entourage. Paul is grieved to report to Timothy (II Timothy 4:10) that "Demas, having loved this present world, has deserted me…" That is what happens when we love the world and the things of the world. You cannot have both on the same throne.
Jesus tells us in Luke 12:15, "…Beware, and be on your guard against every form of greed; for not even when one has an abundance does his life consist of his possessions." We can own things, but things better not own us.

It is easy enough to get so emotionally attached to our things that we do not want to part with them or give them away. The greater our love for our things, the more tightly we grip them. The great holocaust survivor Corrie Ten Boom often spoke these words of wisdom, "Hold loosely to the things of this life, so that if God requires them of you, it will be easy to let them go."

What was the rich, young ruler's obstacle to following Jesus? "But when the young man heard this statement, he went away grieving; for he was one who owned much property (Matthew 19:22)." He didn't own his possessions. His possessions owned him. And they would not let go of him.

If your find that your things own and control you, Caution Light #2 is flashing and you may indeed be involved in an illicit love affair with the world that can destroy your pure and holy relationship to your bride groom, Jesus.

Examining Our Possessions

Caution Light #3

We are falling in love with the world…when worry about losing our things is disrupting our inner peace.

Recent times have certainly given us all ample opportunity to discern if worry about material loss has been disrupting our inner peace. When times are good, we may never even notice Caution Light #3, but when retirement funds plummet, the values of our real estate is in a free fall and our business revenues are off substantially, all this can reveal a love for the world and the things of the world that we may have never really noticed.

Paul reminds us that our financial condition should have nothing to do with our inner peace and contentment in life. He says in Philippians 4:11-12, "Not that I speak from want, for I have learned be content in whatever circumstances I am. I know how to get along with humble means, and I also know how to live in prosperity; in any and every circumstance I have learned the secret of being filled and going hungry, both of having abundance and suffering need."

Being content when you have a lot is quite easy, but being content with less or much less than we have grown comfortable with can be very unsettling and reveal the actual depth of our affection for things of this world.

If you have placed your faith in your things instead of the One who has provided those things, you are in danger. Hebrews 13:5 points this out clearly, "Make sure that your character is free from the love of money, being content with what you have; for He Himself has said, 'I will never desert you, nor will I ever forsake you.'"

If we were stripped of all our worldly possessions and stood penniless, would we still be content and filled with inner peace, confident that our loving Father is still on the throne and will never, ever forsake us?

If you are struggling with a disquieted spirit as you worry over your "net worth" falling and your cash flow shrinking, Caution Light #3 is flashing and you may indeed be involved in an illicit love affair with the world that can destroy your pure and holy relationship to your bride groom, Jesus.

Caution Light #4

We are falling in love with the world…when our longing to be there is diminished by our affection for what we have here.

Mrs. Jones asked her eight year old Sunday school class, "How many of you would like to go to Heaven?" Every child in the class raised his hand except Billy. Mrs. Jones asked curiously, "Billy, don't you want to go to Heaven?" He replied, "Sure I do, I just thought you were taking up a bus load right now!" Billy was glad to go to Heaven, just not right now.

When I was a teenager my grandmother had a heart attack and fell into unconsciousness. Her four daughters (one was my mother) got together and made the decision for the doctors to insert a pacemaker to keep her alive. I remember to this day how furious my grandmother was when she awoke in the hospital and realized that she was still here. She so longed to go to be with the Lord that the life saving intervention of a pacemaker only prevented her from getting where she longed to go. My grandmother's unhappy reaction to still being here is etched permanently in my mind.

I am reminded of what Paul said in II Corinthians 5:8, "prefer rather to be absent from the body and to be at home with the Lord." If you were given the choice today, would you prefer to go be with the Lord or would you prefer to stay here? Are you more like Billy or my grandmother?

If you have nothing more than a casual interest in being there, Caution Light #4 is flashing and you may indeed be involved in an illicit love affair with the world that can destroy your pure and holy relationship to your bride groom, Jesus.

The alluring appeal of the world and the things of the world are very subtle and can sneak up on any of us at any time and begin wrapping its insidious tentacles around us and before we even realize we are trapped, we are overcome. This is the very thing the parable of the seeds describes in Matthew 13:22, "And the one on whom seed was sown among the thorns, this is the man who hears the word, and the worry of the world and the deceitfulness of wealth choke the word, and it becomes unfruitful."

As we continue to live in this materialistic culture of ours, may we all keep our eyes carefully peeled for these four caution lights so we might not unintentionally end up becoming an illicit lover of the world and the things of the world. Hebrews 12:1b-2a challenges us, "Let us also lay aside every encumbrance and the sin which so easily entangles us, and let us run with endurance the race that is set before us, fixing our eyes on Jesus, the author and perfecter of (our) faith…." May this be so for all of us.

Examining Our Possessions

Life Application Questions

1. What is your initial reaction to the video?

_____

_____

_____

_____

2. We are told that God "so loved the world" in John 3:16, but then John tells us to not "love the world" in I John 2:15. How do we explain this apparent contradiction?

_____

_____

_____

_____

3. Ecclesiastes 5:10 says, "Whoever loves money never has money enough; whoever loves wealth is never satisfied with his income." How in our affluent, materialistic society are we encouraged to never be satisfied with what we have? What can we do about it?

_____

_____

_____

_____

4. Jesus warns us, "...Beware, and be on your guard against every form of greed; for not even when one has an abundance does his life consist of his possessions" (Luke 12:15). Make a list of all the areas of your life in which you might be faced with one form of greed or another. What can you do to avoid being infected with greed in any of these areas?

_____

_____

_____

_____

5. Corrie Ten Boom told us to hold loosely to the things of this life, so that if God requires them of you, it will be easy to let go of them. This is easy to say, but how can we actually, consciously live this way on a daily basis? What do we need to be doing to keep our hands from gripping too tightly to our possessions?

    _____

    _____

    _____

    _____

6. Philippians 4:11-12 says, "Not that I speak from want, for I have learned to be content in whatever circumstances I am. I know how to get along with humble means, and I also know how to live in prosperity; in any and every circumstance I have learned the secret of being filled and going hungry, both of having abundance and suffering need." What is Paul's secret to contentment? It cannot be material things because he was content with or without them.

    _____

    _____

    _____

    _____

7. When we find ourselves fearful about the loss of our material things or current lifestyle, what should that tell us about our relationship to our Father?

    _____

    _____

    _____

    _____

8. Can you relate more to little Billy in the Sunday school class or Jay's grandmother in your attitude about going to be with Jesus? What can we do to make us more excited about what is still yet to come than we are about what is already here?

    _____

    _____

    _____

    _____

Examining Our Possessions

9. Matthew 13:22 says, "And the one on whom seed was sown among the thorns, this is the
who hears the word, and the worry of the world and the deceitfulness of wealth choke the
and it becomes unfruitful." In what ways can wealth/material possessions be deceitful? Wh
we do to make sure we are not deceived by them and therefore making the Word unfruitful
lives?

_____

_____

_____

_____

10. On a scale of 1-10 rank how brightly you think the four caution lights might be flashing in yc
personal life.

(1 – not flashing at all: 10 – flashing brightly!)

Caution Light #1: (we are never quite satisfied with what we have) _____

Caution Light #2: (things we own end up owning us) _____

Caution Light #3: (worry about losing our things is disrupting our inner peace) _____

Caution Light #4: (our longing to be there is diminished by our affection for
                                    what we have here) _____

• 63

Examining Our Possessions - Additional Food for Thought/Home Study Material

Being Poor in Spirit While Rich in Things

In America, we live in the richest nation in the world. So, the idea of being poor in spirit while bein surrounded with degrees of material prosperity and opulence that relatively few have ever enjoyed presents us with both an extraordinary challenge and opportunity that can either prove to be powerful or destructive depending on how we choose to respond to it. So, we need to ask, "How are we supposed to be poor in spirit while being rich in things?"

First, we must understand what the phrase poor in spirit means. This phrase is found in Jesus' Sermon on the Mount (Matthew 5:3). It is the first of the eight beatitudes that all begin with blesse which means literally "happy, fortunate or blissful."

We need to understand the actual meaning of these words. The word poor comes from the Greek word that means "to shrink, cower or cringe," as beggars often did in that day. Classical Greek us the word to refer to a person who was reduced to total destitution. One who was crouched in the corner begging, with one hand reaching out and the other covering his face in shame. This term is not just used to simply mean poor, but begging poor. This is the same word that is used in Luke 16:20 to describe Lazarus.

The Greek word normally used for poverty is a different word entirely and is used to describe the poor widow Jesus observed giving her offering at the Temple. She had very little, but she still had two small copper coins (Luke 21:2). The words "in spirit" focus not on material poverty, but on spiritual poverty. In the same way that people are begging poor materially, here Jesus is describin begging poor spiritually.

Being poor in spirit comes when we recognize our total spiritual destitution and our complete dependence on God. There is no saving resource in us. There is nothing that we can offer of valu We are left begging poor. And our only recourse is to reach out our sin-sick hands and beg God f mercy and grace.

The story of the Pharisee and the tax collector in Luke 18:10-14 NIV is the classic contrast betwee one who was rich in spirit and one who was poor in spirit. Jesus said, "Two men went up to the temple to pray, one a Pharisee and the other a tax collector. The Pharisee stood up and prayed about himself: 'God, I thank you that I am not like other men—robbers, evildoers, adulterers—or even like this tax collector. I fast twice a week and give a tenth of all I get.' "But the tax collector stood at a distance. He would not even look up to heaven, but beat his breast and said, 'God, hav mercy on me, a sinner.' "I tell you that this man, rather than the other, went home justified before God. For everyone who exalts himself will be humbled, and he who humbles himself will be exalted

We do not like the idea of admitting that we are poor in spirit. It is contrary to our human nature. fight against acknowledging it. A good example of this resistance to admit a poverty of spirit is fou in the great hymn "At the Cross." It has a line in the first verse that says, "Should He devote that

cred head for such a worm as I?" David uses this term "worm" in one of his Messianic Psalms (22:6)
V "But I am a worm and not a man, scorned by men and despised by the people." So, this term is a
blically inspired word describing Jesus on the cross.

owever, the thought of being a worm is so repulsive in our modern culture that most current hymnals
ave changed the original words to the song from "for such a worm as I" to "for such a one as I" or
or sinners such as I." We just do not like to admit that we are spiritual worms. But in contrast to the
oliness of God, a worm is a very accurate description of where we stand with God spiritually.

he joy of it all is that God so loved us worms that He sent His son to redeem us so we could experience
spiritual metamorphosis and be changed from a worm to a son.

o, being poor in spirit is not about how God views me or even how other people view me, it is about
ow I view me.

he best way to understand what poor in spirit means is to look at how men viewed their own spiritual
chness" when they came into the presence of God.

- Isaiah said, "Woe to me… I am a man of unclean lips" (Isaiah 6:5 nasb).

- Gideon said, "O Lord, how shall I deliver Israel? Behold, my family is the least in Manasseh, and I am the youngest in my father's house. (Judges 6:15 nasb).

- Jeremiah said, "Behold, I do not know how to speak, because I am a youth" (Jeremiah 1:6 nasb).

- Moses said, "Who am I" (Exodus 3:11 nasb).

- David said, "Who am I, O Lord God, and what is my house, that you have brought me thus far?"(II Samuel 7:18 esv).

- Peter said, "Depart from me; for I am a sinful man" (Luke 5:8 nkjv).

- Paul said, "I am the foremost of all (sinners)" (I Timothy 1:15 nasb).

overty of spirit is a personal awareness and recognition before God that there is nothing in us or about
s that warrants any sense of self-sufficiency or spiritual "richness" that might be applied to our credit.
Ve are all at our core begging poor spiritually.

t. Francis de Sales wrote a book entitled, "Introduction to the Devout Life," [trans. John K. Ryan
Garden City, NY: Doubleday Image Books, 1972, pp. 161-167)] that is a series of hypothetical letters to
new convert he calls Philothea ("Lover of God"). In one of his letters de Sales addresses the issue of

Examining Our Possessions - Additional Food for Thought/Home Study Material

material possessions and the attitude a Christian who is poor in spirit ought to have towards them. His counsel is quite profound especially since it was written over 400 years ago.

> Blessed are the poor in Spirit, for theirs is the Kingdom of Heaven." Accursed, then, are the rich in spirit for the misery of hell is their portion.

> A man is rich in spirit if his mind is filled with riches or set on riches. The kingfisher shapes nest like an apple, leaving only a little opening at the top, builds it on the seashore, and ma it so solid and tight that although waves sweep over it the water cannot get inside. Keepin always on the top of the waves, they remain surrounded by the sea and are on the sea, an yet are masters of it.

> The Poverty of Spirit to be Observed in the Midst of Riches

> Your heart, dear Philothea, must in like manner be open to heaven alone and impervious to riches and all other transitory things. Whatever part of them you may possess, you must keep your heart free from the slightest affection for them. Always keep it above them and while it may be surrounded by riches it remains apart from riches and master over them. Do not allow this heavenly spirit to become captive to earthly goods. Let it always remain superior to them and over them, not in them.

> There is a difference between having poison and being poisoned. Pharmacists keep almos every kind of poison in stock for use on various occasions, yet they are not themselves poisoned because they merely have it in their shops and not in their bodies. So also you c possess riches without being poisoned by them if you merely keep them in your home and purse and not in your heart…

> Unfortunately, Philothea, no one is ready ever to admit that he is avaricious ("has an insatia greed for riches"). Everyone denies having so base and mean a heart. One man excuses himself on the score that he has to take care of his children - that this fact puts him under obligation to them, and that prudence requires that he be a man of property. He never has too much; he always finds need for more.

> The most avaricious men not only deny they are avaricious but even think in their conscienc they are not such. Avarice is a raging fever that makes itself all the harder to detect the mo violent and burning it is.

> Moses saw the sacred fire that burned but did not consume the bush. On the contrary, avarice is a profane, unholy fire that both consumes and devours but does not consume an avaricious man…

How to Practice Genuine Poverty Although Really Rich

Dear Philothea, I would like to instill into your heart both wealth and poverty together, that is, great care and also great contempt for temporal things.

Have greater care than the worldly men do to make your property profitable and fruitful. Princes' gardeners are more careful and faithful in cultivating and beautifying the gardens in their charge than if they were their own property. Why is this? Undoubtedly it is because they see the gardens as the property of princes and kings to whom they want to make themselves acceptable by their services.

Philothea, our possessions are not our own. God has given them to us to cultivate and He wants us to make them fruitful and profitable. Hence we perform an acceptable service by taking good care of them. It must be a greater and finer care than that which worldly men have for their property. They labor only out of self-love and we must labor out of love of God…

Therefore let us exercise this gracious care of preserving and even of increasing our temporal goods whatever occasions present themselves as so far as our condition in life requires, for God desires us to do so out of love for Him But be on guard so that self-love does not deceive you. Sometimes it counterfeits the love of God so closely that one might say it is the same thing. In order that it may not trick you and that care of temporal possessions may not degenerate to avarice…we must practice real poverty in the midst of all the goods and riches God has given us.

Frequently give up some of your property by giving it with a generous heart to the poor. To give away what we have is to impoverish ourselves in proportion as we give, and the more we give the poorer we become… until such time as God shall restore it to us we remain the poorer in the amount we have given. Oh, how holy and how rich is the poverty brought on by giving alms!

There are two "ditches" on each side of this narrow road of being poor in spirit while being rich in things that must be avoided. One ditch to avoid is not letting our material possessions deceive us into becoming rich in spirit – "thinking more highly of ourselves than we ought" (Romans 12:3). The other ditch to avoid is not letting our lack of material possessions deceive us into concluding that having material possessions is somehow carnal and unspiritual – leading us to becoming rich in spirit because we have little.

The centerline on this road, simply stated, is to be spiritually poor while being materially generous. So, the more begging poor we become spiritually and the richer and more generous we become materially, the more useful we will become to His Majesty, the King.

Food for Thought Questions

1. For you personally, what was the most striking comment de Sales made?

_____

_____

_____

_____

2. According to de Sales, what is the proper purpose for growing one's wealth?

_____

_____

_____

_____

3. De Sales likens material possessions to poison, but tells us how to avoid being poisoned by them while we possess them. How effective have you been in avoiding being poisoned by possessions?

_____

_____

_____

_____

69

Examining Our Possessions - Additional Food for Thought/Home Study Material

Slave or Master?

The Wisdom Books in the Bible reference a quite unusual occurrence that because it is mentioned multiple times must have at least occasionally happened - a slave becoming a ruler. Here are three references:

> "Under three things the earth quakes, and under four, it cannot bear up: Under a slave when he becomes king…" (Proverbs 30:21-22a).

> "Luxury is not fitting for a fool, much less for a slave to rule over princes" (Proverbs 19:10).

> "I have seen slaves riding on horses and princes walking like slaves on the land" (Ecclesiastes 10:7).

All three of these passages suggest this picture of a slave becoming the ruler due to some strange twisted irony as being completely wrong and even dangerous.

I think we can make an important application to these "slave turned ruler" passages that applies to us today even though none of us are slaveholders - that being that our material possessions are our modern day slaves of which we are to be the rulers.

The question that we need to ask is, "In my world, who is the servant and who is the master?" The answer may not be as clear or as obvious as we might like to think. Let me ask you the question this way, "Do you own your possessions or do your possessions own you? Are you the servant or are you the master?

Let me share a personal illustration. Many years ago, I wanted to buy two horses for my young daughters to ride. So I went out and bought two older horses. I was so excited to be the proud owner of two new horses…I thought.

What I learned was that these horses I now owned needed to be watered everyday and the new barn that I built to shelter them had no running water, so I had to fill up buckets of water at the house and carry the water over to the barn (a very long walk). Two horses drink a lot of water! That lasted a short while until I paid to have a water line run to the barn. I also realized that these horses I owned needed to be given hay every day. So I had to buy hay, which meant I had to buy an old pickup truck to haul the hay to the barn. Then I had to load it in the loft and then go to the barn twice a day and throw some of it into their mangers.

Then the real shock! These horses indiscriminately redeposited all the hay and grain I fed them right back onto the stall floor. Adult horses and they weren't potty trained! And guess who got to regularly shovel it out of the stalls and haul it away!

ter one winter of that, I had had enough and I built a shelter in the pasture so they could stay in the field
ar round. This solved one problem and created two new ones. Now I had to hook a hose to the water
e to get it out to their water tank which would routinely freeze in the winter so I would have to go out
th my crow bar each day and break the ice so the horses could drink. I finally spent more money to run
ectricity out to the shelter to put a heater in the tank so it wouldn't freeze. I still had to take the hose back
the house after each fill up to keep it from freezing and breaking. I also had to now haul the hay from the
rn loft out to the field.

dmittedly, I am a little slow, but one day it hit me. I didn't own these horses, these horses owned me. I
d become their servant and they had become my master. The country song says it best, "I know what I
as feeling, but what was I thinking?"

ou may laugh at my youthful ignorance, but I fear that all of us may be guilty to one degree or another of
e same folly. We think we are accumulating "servants" only to discover that these "servants" often end
becoming our masters. The more we accumulate the more our lives are consumed with taking care of
ur servants – cars, houses, clothes, "toys," investments, businesses – take your pick. Let me ask you,
Do you really own them or do they, in fact, own you?"

am a businessman and there are times I must honestly confess, I feel more like my business owns me
an that I own my business? I work endless hours for it, caring for it, managing it, paying attention to
very detail of it, making sure it is healthy and growing, nursing it when it is sick. I also need to care for my
mployees and as every businessman learns sooner or later when things get tight the employees get paid
efore the owner does. Tell me again, who's the owner and who's the servant?

cannot think of any kind of asset that if left unattended will not eventually end up becoming a costly
ability. Don't service your car and see what happens. Your house is constantly in need of your attention
nd your money to keep it from falling down around you. Your clothes don't wash, iron and hang
emselves up. Even your children and your spouse, if you do not invest huge amounts of everything into
em, will eventually become a major liability to you.

think one of the greatest delusions we often fall prey to is the folly of thinking that the wealthier we can
ecome materially, the more freedom we will have. It has been my personal experience and professional
bservation that it is not at all that black and white. In fact, in many cases, the opposite is true. Often the
ealthier a person becomes the more enslaved he is to caring for and attending to all his "servants" and
e less flexibility and freedom he actually has – emotionally, spiritually, and physically for really important
ursuits and priorities of life. It is a trade off of one freedom for another that often leaves us less free after
ach trade.

Examining Our Possessions - Additional Food for Thought/Home Study Material

It may just be that the freest person in the world is not the mega-wealthy individual, but is actua the person who owns nothing – who has no material masters that are demanding huge amount his time, his attention, and his physical and emotional energy to care for them.

Consider this story: A businessman was at the pier of a small coastal Mexican village when a sm boat with just one fisherman docked. Inside the small boat were several large yellowfin tuna. The businessman complimented the Mexican on the quality of his fish and asked how long it took to catch them. The Mexican replied only a little while.

The businessman then asked why he didn't stay out longer and catch more fish? The Mexican s he had enough to support his family's immediate needs. The businessman then asked, "But wha you do with the rest of your time?"
The Mexican fisherman said, "I sleep late, fish a little, play with my children, take a siesta with my wife Maria and stroll into the village each evening where I sip wine and play guitar with my amigo have a full and busy life, señor."

The businessman scoffed, "I am a Harvard MBA and I could help you. You should spend more ti fishing and with the proceeds buy a bigger boat. With the proceeds from the bigger boat you co buy several boats; eventually you would have a fleet of fishing boats. Instead of selling your catch a middleman, you would sell directly to the processor and eventually open your own cannery. Yo would control the product, processing and distribution. You would need to leave this small coast fishing village and move to Mexico City, then LA and eventually New York City where you would r your expanding enterprise."

The Mexican fisherman asked, "But señor, how long will this all take?" To which the businessmar replied, "15-20 years."

"But what then, señor?" The businessman laughed and said, "That's the best part! When the time right you would announce an IPO and sell your company stock to the public and become very ric You would make millions."

"Millions, señor? Then what?" The businessman said, "Then you would retire. Move to a small coastal fishing village where you would sleep late, fish a little, play with your kids, take a siesta wit your wife and stroll to the village in the evenings where you could sip wine and play your guitar wi your amigos."

The fisherman, still smiling, looked up and said, "Isn't that what I'm doing right now?"

As this new year begins, might it not be good for all of us to take a personal inventory of our lives and our material possessions and determine just how much of what we legally "own" actually emotionally, spiritually, and/or financially "owns" us and through some twisted irony we now "see (our) slaves riding on horses (while we are) walking like slaves on the land" (Ecclesiastes 10:7).

Food for Thought Questions

1. What assets have you accumulated that you thought were to be your servants, but have come to realize that they have actually become your master?

   _____

   _____

   _____

   _____

2. Discuss the following statement, "I cannot think of any kind of asset that if left unattended will not eventually end up becoming a costly liability." What assets in your life have you inadvertently allowed to become liabilities in your life?

   _____

   _____

   _____

   _____

3. What lesson(s) did you draw from the story of the Mexican fisherman and the MBA businessman?

   _____

   _____

   _____

   _____

WHO'S IN CHARGE HERE?

Examining Our Possessions - Additional Food for Thought/Home Study Material

For Money…

Recently I attended a conference and one of the main speakers made a passing comment in his presentation that froze me in that moment. He said, "Judas betrayed Jesus for money." I have known all my life that Judas betrayed Jesus for 30 pieces of silver, but for some reason it wasn't until that very moment that I connected that thirty pieces of silver to money – where I have spent most of my professional life. As soon as he made that statement, "Judas betrayed Jesus for money," a mirror appeared before me and I found my own reflection in it and for the first time in my entire life I found myself painfully identifying with Judas.

Over my life I have often related to Peter, too bold and carelessly impetuous, and to Samson, with great strength, but lack of self-control, and even to King Saul, who "played the fool." But never before have I ever seen myself in Judas, the betrayer – until that moment.

The idea continued to nag at me. When I got home I began to study the events surrounding Judas' betrayal. I wanted to know what the word "betray" really meant. It means to "turn someone over to another," the way a police officer would turn over a convict to a prison warden. Has my life or my behavior ever turned Jesus over to be mocked and ridiculed by another because of my hypocritical and self-centered life? Remember Judas didn't kill Jesus, he only set Him up to be killed by others. Have I ever set Jesus up to be "crucified" by others?

I found that Luke (6:16) called Judas a "traitor" – meaning "someone who is false to a duty or an obligation." I was feeling even more uncomfortable at this point. Have I ever been inconsistent in my duty and my obligation to Christ because His will and my will didn't align? Have I abandoned His "ship" for my own because my "ship" looked more profitable? Have I ever been guilty of dereliction of duty to him in my financial dealings?

Okay, maybe I have betrayed Jesus and been a traitor to him on some occasions in my life. But surely I've not been as exceedingly disloyal as Judas was. Judas had his price? In today's dollars, what was Judas' price to sell out Jesus? My study revealed that thirty shekels (pieces) of silver was the standard price of an adult slave (Exodus 21:32). A slave, when bought, would be bound for six years to his owner and then he was to be set free (Exodus 21:2). So, when a man bought a slave, he was in effect prepaying for six years of slave labor. If we assume the current minimum wage as our version of modern day "slave labor" and multiply that by six years of full time work (40 hours x 52 weeks) then in today's dollars Judas sold Jesus out for about $75,000.

I moaned - $75,000? The Lord brought to my mind times when I had indeed been His traitor and betrayer in some of my past financial dealings and sadly it was for a whole lot less than Judas' $75,000. I have been guilty of betraying Jesus for money.

Think about it, have you ever "embellished" your deductions on a tax return in order to pay less in taxes? Have you ever intentionally failed to fully disclose all the pertinent information so as to not lose a sale? Have you ever done a cash transaction and not reported the income? Have you overcharged someone or been undercharged and not corrected the financial error that was in your favor? Have you ever padded your expense account? Have you ever found yourself calculating ways to give less to the Lord by using some creative financial gymnastics to come up with your giving amount? Have you ever skipped worship to work and make more money?

I could go on and eventually hit some nerve in all of us, but I will let the Holy Spirit bring to your mind how you have betrayed Jesus and played the traitor for money just as He has reminded me of my betrayals. I hope you will give Him time to bring those situations to your mind by meditating on this matter for a while.

One final interesting detail in this story; the only Gospel writer that records the actually price of Judas' betrayal is Matthew – the man whose previous career was the patently dishonest financial business of tax collecting. He was well acquainted with lying, stealing and cheating to get more money. Apparently, Matthew wanted us to know all the sordid financial details of Judas' traitorous deed. Maybe he records these details to warn those of us who may have a similar sinful inclination not to fall prey to the same devastating temptation and delusion that Judas did.

Please do not misunderstand what I am saying. I am not suggesting that any of us are some kind of modern day Judas. But when we see even the faintest likeness of Judas' moral and spiritual depravity in us, I think we all should be appropriately humbled and sincerely repentant when we see his pathetic likeness appearing in our personal or professional lives.

What is most sad about the story of Judas and for us when we emulate him is that Judas didn't really betray Jesus for money; Judas betrayed himself for money. And in the end, he lost his money, he lost his life and he lost his eternity. It was an entirely bad deal for him and it will likewise be a bad deal for us too whenever we, even in the smallest ways, choose to betray Jesus for money.

Examining Our Possessions - Additional Food for Thought/Home Study Material

Food for Thought Questions

1. Have you ever been able to relate to Judas up to this point in your life?

   _____
   _____
   _____
   _____

2. Ask the Lord to bring to your mind ways in which you have you been personally guilty of betraying Jesus for money. Write down what He brings to your mind. Are you prepared to make a commitment to Jesus, never to betray Him again in these ways?

   _____
   _____
   _____
   _____

3. Discuss the following statement. "Judas didn't really betray Jesus for money, he betrayed himself for money." In what ways is this true and would it be equally true of us if we were to play the traitor in our business and financial dealings?

   _____
   _____
   _____
   _____

Controlling Our Lifestyle

Living on Less

Recently I received an email with the subject line, "You can live on less when you have more to live for." This statement so struck me that I literally stopped my expeditious handling of all my emails and just pondered this profound and thought-provoking statement. "You can live on less when you have more to live for."

This is not a statement describing an involuntary "belt-tightening" when economic circumstances force one to reduce a preferred lifestyle. It is talking about someone who chooses to voluntarily reduce his current lifestyle – a willing reduction.

Routinely, one of the primary objectives in planning for those who have surplus cash flow and excess wealth is to ensure that they are able to maintain their current lifestyle while doing all their inheritance charitable planning. The key word here is "maintain." In other words, "I am willing to be as charitable possible with my "wealth" as long as it does not negatively impact my current lifestyle.

But this statement suggests that there might actually be some reasons why a person would want to reduce his rate of personal consumption (what we call the "burn rate") to intentionally "live on less."

So what might happen that would lead a person who could live on more – much more – to happily and willingly choose to live on less? This quote tells us. They have found something "more to live for" – something that is more valuable and more fulfilling to them than self-consumption.

As I pondered this statement, I asked myself, "What would it take for me or anyone else to willingly choose to live on less?" I concluded that in order to choose to live on less there would have to be a change in one or more of these three areas – (1.) one's Perspective, (2.) one's Priorities, and/or (3.) one's Purpose.

A Change in Perspective

I travel a lot and in order to avoid feeling "claustrophobic" on the plane, I always try to get an aisle seat but on occasion, I find myself "trapped" in a window seat. If there is any redemption to a window seat it is the view. I must confess that there is nothing that gives me a more realistic perspective of life than looking at the world from 35,000 feet.

Elevation does seem to give us a substantially different perspective on the "things of earth." If we could pile up all of Bill Gate's and Warren Buffet's "stuff" in one place, it might not even be noticeable from the viewpoint of 35,000 feet. How much more insignificant are things if viewed from the footstool of Heaven. If a man were to see the trappings of his current lifestyle from the perspective of Heaven, he might just conclude there is undoubtedly something "more to live for" than the insignificant and temporary creature comforts of his current lifestyle.

Matthew 13:44-46 gives us a picture of what happens when someone's perspective changes. Jesus said, "The kingdom of heaven is like treasure hidden in a field. When a man found it, he hid it again, and then in his joy went and sold all he had and bought that field. Again, the kingdom of heaven is like a merchant looking for fine pearls. When he found one of great value, he went away and sold everything he had and bought it."

Their perception of the value of their current possessions was totally redefined when they discovered something they perceived to be of far greater worth. There is an old riddle, "Do you know how to get a bone out of a dog's mouth?" The answer is, "Offer him a bone with more meat on it."

We will gladly "live on less" when our perspective is reoriented and reveals something "more to live for." By downsizing, we would actually be upgrading!

A Change in Priorities

We all have a list of priorities. They are seldom put in writing and placed on the refrigerator, but we all have them stored away somewhere in the recesses of our consciousness. When given a choice between two options, our list of priorities kicks in and we choose the one highest on the list. This is true with our time and our treasures.

If your child has a ball game and you also have an opportunity to go play golf with your best friends, which you choose will demonstrate your priorities. If you had to choose between helping your child with their college expenses or buying a new car, your pre-set priorities will determine which choice you make. And, likewise, when given the choice between deploying your material resources for Kingdom purposes or buying a bigger home or the latest luxury car, your priorities will determine your choice.

We recently were hired by a younger couple who had done extremely well professionally and financially. The husband and wife came from nothing and as their businesses grew and their income skyrocketed, so did their lifestyle. They found themselves with an extravagant home, the newest and most expensive vehicles, and all the toys and trappings of a family who had "made it."

But something happened to this couple along the way. God began to burden them with the call of the great commission and the need to get the gospel out while there was still time – before Jesus' return. And quite apart from any influence by me, the husband had already made the decision that he wanted to become one of the greatest Christian philanthropists in history. In order to do this, they have already begun to cut their lifestyle consumption by multiples in order to have more available to deploy for Kingdom work. They are selling their "mansion" and moving into a modest home. They are buying cheaper used cars and intend to drive them until they cannot be driven anymore. His goal now is to build as many businesses as he can and grow them as much as he can so he can give as much as possible to the Kingdom during the rest of his life. Talk about a change in priorities!

For a man to choose to "live on less" it will require a radical reordering of existing priorities and these newly reordered priorities likely will reveal to him that there is much "more to live for."

Controlling Our Lifestyle

A Change in Purpose

In one of my slideshow presentations I ask the question, "What on earth am I doing with all this we... I think it is an imminently practical and important question that each of us needs to answer. And h... answer that question will be reflected by what we choose to do with our material possessions. Did give us excess material possessions to increase our lifestyle or to increase our Kingdom impact? [our Father provide us with surplus resources so we could be "rich in lifestyle" or so we could be "ri... good deeds" (I Timothy 6:18)?

I can think of no more powerful example of this statement, "You can live on less when you have mo... live for," than what is vividly demonstrated in the life and death of Jesus himself. II Corinthians 8:9 t... us, "For you know the grace of our Lord Jesus Christ, that though He was rich, yet for your sake H... became poor, that you through His poverty might become rich."

Jesus was the richest "man" in the universe and yet facing a divine purpose that collided with His e... place in Heaven, He willingly "humbled Himself" and "made Himself nothing" (Philippians 2:6-8) and... came to a dirty, sin-filled, remote planet to accomplish this divine purpose. He downsized from a th... in Heaven to a cross on Calvary.

Jesus was pursuing a purpose that required Him to radically reduce His preferred lifestyle in order to carry out a grand and noble purpose – the redemption of the entire human race.

I think none of us can escape the probing question that if Jesus, being rich, became poor for us so we could be rich, what does He intend for us to do with those riches we have gained from His volur... poverty? We need to soberly ponder this question.

For a man to choose to "live on less" it will require a radical reorientation of his life purpose that will r... to him that there is indeed a greater life purpose that will give him even "more to live for."

"You can live on less when you have more to live for." Maybe each of us ought to humbly reconsider current perspective, our current priorities, and our current purpose. It may be that if we honestly ass... these three areas of our lives and humbly attempt to align them with the perspective, priorities, and purpose of Christ, we might just find to our surprise that we will be glad to "live on less" because in ... doing we have found "more to live for" – much more.

Life Application Questions

1. What was your initial reaction to the statement, "You can live on less when you have more to live for?"

_____

_____

_____

_____

2. In Matthew 13:44-46 Jesus gives us an illustration, "The kingdom of heaven is like treasure hidden in a field. When a man found it, he hid it again, and then in his joy went and sold all he had and bought that field. Again, the kingdom of heaven is like a merchant looking for fine pearls. When he found one of great value, he went away and sold everything he had and bought it." What would be the "treasure" or the "pearl of great value" that would motivate you to sell everything you possess in order to have it?

_____

_____

_____

_____

3. Here is a list of typical life-priorities. Put them in your order of priority.

   a. Job/Career   _____
   b. Spouse   _____
   c. Children   _____
   d. Entertainment   _____
   e. Recreation/Sports _____
   f. Friends   _____
   g. Money   _____
   h. Success   _____
   i. Image   _____
   j. Power   _____

   Now, give this same list to your spouse and then to your children (or friends) and ask them to list what they see your order of priorities to be. Compare your list to their list. What might you learn from this exercise?

_____

_____

_____

_____

Controlling Our Lifestyle

4. How did the story of the young, very successful couple who was substantially downsizing so they could give more away impact you?

_____
_____
_____
_____

How does it make you feel to know Jesus willingly downsized from a throne in Heaven to a cross on Calvary for you?

_____
_____
_____
_____

II Corinthians 8:9 tells us, "For you know the grace of our Lord Jesus Christ, that though He was rich, yet for your sake He became poor, that you through His poverty might become rich."

If Jesus, being rich, became poor for you so that you could be rich, what does He intend for you to do with those riches that you have gained from His voluntary poverty?

_____
_____
_____
_____

How does your life-perspective, life-priority and life-purpose line up with the perspectives, priorities and purposes of Christ?

_____
_____
_____
_____

What are you going to do about these discrepancies?

_____
_____
_____
_____

For you personally, what would the "more to live for" have to be for you to gladly choose to "live on less"?

_____

_____

_____

_____

Controlling Our Lifestyle - Additional Food for Thought/Home Study Material

Are You Trading Up or Trading Down?

Are you a day trader in the stock market? Probably not. However, I would suggest that all of us day traders. We have spent most of our lives trading one thing for another. As a follower of Jesu I think we must all carefully consider what we choose to trade away and what we get back in the trade. It may well be that in light of what you read here, you might want to modify your current trading strategy.

Before we can fully determine whether we are actually trading up or trading down we need to identify the three worlds of life:

The first World is what I call **The Inanimate World**
(The World of Things/The Lower World)

The second World is what I call **The Human World**
(The World of People/The Middle World)

The third World is what I call **The Spiritual World**
(The World of God/The Higher World)

These three worlds are not exclusive or unconnected. In fact, we exist in all three simultaneously. God has given us clear directions to help us understand these three worlds and how to enjoy the greatest possible benefit from each of them. However, as seems to always be the case, we are r naturally inclined towards a healthy balance between these three worlds.

Our lives begin with only a limited awareness of the Human World and no awareness of the other two worlds. However, it doesn't take long before a child becomes quite captivated with the Inanimate World. (Think of a child and his/her toys.) As we mature we discover that we can trade assets in our Human World (our time and our abilities) to acquire possessions in the Inanimate W that appeal to us and that we believe will give us pleasure.

When we choose to pursue making money or getting rich, we simply agree to trade what we possess in the Human World (our lives) for the acquisition of things in the Inanimate World (cash, electronics, cars, house, businesses, etc.). In so doing we are trading what is life for what is lifele We are trading down what we possess in the Human World to acquire something we want in the Inanimate World.

So, in the pursuit of inanimate objects, man willingly sacrifices some portion of his life to gain then

We may picture a man getting fatter and fatter as his accumulated wealth increases, but a more accurate image would be to see him as becoming more scrawny and emaciated as he continues to trade more and more of his life in the Human World for what is lifeless in the Inanimate World.

The story of Howard Hughes is just one of hundreds of tragic examples of what happens when a man sacrifices all he has in the Human World to gain what he wants in the Inanimate World. He died a drug addicted recluse who at 6' 2" weighed only 90 pounds with a scraggly beard that hung to his waste, two inch long fingernails and toe nails that resembled cork screws. He chose to trade down. And in the trade he sacrificed life for things.

Think of this idea of trading in the context of growing a garden. The portion of your life you devote to growing that garden has been traded down to a harvest of inanimate produce. In a very real sense, part of you has been turned into a potato or a cucumber. (Rather a humbling thought, isn't it?) Now, if you eat the potato or cucumber, you immediately turn the lifeless vegetable back into life again (your life). But if you sell it and turn it into money and put the money in the bank, you have become the money in the bank. Earl Pierce called this conversion of life to things "coined man." Ravi Zacharias calls it "congealed life."

Land, buildings, cars, investments, gold, and silver are all part of the Inanimate World as well. In our pursuit of them we trade down the life we possess in the Human World to acquire what is lifeless in the Inanimate World.

Accumulating surplus possessions is an activity exclusively practiced by humans. Animals do not do this. Animals, at most, only store up enough to meet their current and short term future needs. Squirrels, for example, will store up enough nuts for the entire winter season. Ants do the same (Proverbs 6:6-8). But an ant does not store up enough for many winters to come. A squirrel does not try to corner the market on nuts and then resell them at a profit to other less creative and farsighted squirrels.

Do you remember in Luke 12:19 the comment of the rich farmer who was going to build bigger barns to store his bumper crop? He said, "…Soul, you have many goods laid up for many years to come; take your ease, eat, drink and be merry." Contrast his comment with what Jesus told those listening to His sermon on the Mount, "Look at the birds of the air, that they do not sow, neither do they reap, nor gather into barns, and yet your heavenly Father feeds them. Are you not worth much more than they?" (Matthew 6:26). What is this telling us about trading down?

This inherent instinct of man to accumulate surplus wealth is proof that man did not evolve from the animals, but was created by the Owner of all things. Man has a natural, divine instinct to be an owner/heir and an accumulator. The problem is that in our fallen condition, this divine instinct of ownership most often degenerates into avarice, pride and self-destruction.

So, we need to ask, "Can My Congealed Life Ever be Recovered?"

Controlling Our Lifestyle - Additional Food for Thought/Home Study Material

The good news is, "Yes!" You can redeem the life you traded to acquire lifeless assets by now us
those lifeless things for a good purpose in the Human World or the Spiritual World. You can bring
them back to life again.

Ebenezer Scrooge is a great example of a man who had reduced his life to an impressive balance
sheet of lifeless things in the Inanimate World. Yet, unknown to him, in the human world he was s
pitiful and impoverished and in the Spiritual World he was altogether dead. Thankfully, through the
three visitations, he finally realized his poor trading practices and gladly began resurrecting part of
lost life by deploying his inanimate possessions back into the Human World using them to bless a
assist his fellow human beings, most notably, Tiny Tim.

Unlike Scrooge, King David wanted to not just trade up some of his inanimate possessions, to the
Human World, he wanted to trade them up to the Spiritual World. I Chronicles 21 tells the story.
Ornan wanted to give David everything he needed to offer a sacrifice to the Lord. But King David s
to Ornan in verse 24, "No, but I will surely buy it for the full price; for I will not take what is yours fo
Lord, or offer a burnt offering which costs me nothing."

David wanted to give something of himself, his own life, to God. He did not want to give somethin
of Ornan's life to God. So David took his "congealed life" to buy the land, the wood, and the neede
animals and in so doing he offered a part of himself to the Lord in the sacrifice. He traded up.

Should we not be reminded of what Jesus said about trading up and not trading down? In Matthe
6:19-20 He tells us, allow me to paraphrase, "Do not (trade down) for yourself treasures on earth i
the Inanimate World..., but trade up for yourselves treasures in heaven in the Spiritual World...."

I think we need to ask, "What about those to whom God has given the power to make more wealt
than they need to live on as in Deuteronomy 8:18?" For those whom God has empowered to be
wealth makers, I would suggest that they should indeed do so with all the power that God has giv
them. But the critical question must be asked, "Be a wealth maker for what purpose?"

If these gifted wealth makers use their surplus, accumulated, inanimate assets (cash, investment
accounts, real estate holdings, business interests, personal property, etcetera.) their success has
provided to them for Kingdom purposes – they will be trading up (trading human life for spiritual life
they use them to meet their own physical needs or the physical needs of others – they will be tradi
even (trading human life for human life). And if they retain their inanimate, surplus possessions in t
current state for their own pleasure and security – they will have traded down (trading human life fc
no life at all).

The objective is clear. Our fundamental motivation and primary purpose for making surplus wealth
to trade up with it.

ou already have accumulated surplus, inanimate wealth, let me command you based upon I
nothy 6:17-19 to trade up (human life for spiritual life).

ommand those who are rich in this present world not to be arrogant nor to put their hope in wealth,
ich is so uncertain, but to put their hope in God, who richly provides us with everything for our
joyment, Command them to do good, to be rich in good deeds, and to be generous and willing to
are. In this way they will lay up treasure for themselves as a firm foundation for the coming age, so
at they may take hold of the life that is truly life."

ou have not accumulated surplus, inanimate wealth, let me encourage you based upon Hebrews
:5, to be content with what you have and not be tempted to trade down (human life for lifeless
ngs).

says, "Let your character be free from the love of money, being content with what you have; for He
mself has said, 'I will never desert you, nor will I ever forsake you…'"

ay we all be careful not to be seduced by the lie of the great deceiver that the best of life can be
quired in trading down. Be sure the best of life (in both this life and the one yet to come) will always
found in trading up.

Controlling Our Lifestyle - Additional Food for Thought/Home Study Material

Food for Thought Questions

1. What is so revolutionary about the idea of trading our human life in order to possess inanim
things?

_____

_____

_____

_____

2. What can we learn about wealth and its impact on its possessors from the story of Howard
Hughes?

_____

_____

_____

_____

3. Read I Chronicles 21 to determine how King David converted something from the inanimate
world to the spiritual world?

_____

_____

_____

_____

Controlling Our Lifestyle - Additional Food for Thought/Home Study Material

The Numbing Effect

Have you ever been reading a passage in the Bible about the depravity of unbelievers only sudde
to have your face appear on the page before you? This happened to me recently reminding me t
since we are all still fallen creatures (albeit forgiven), to the extent we do not allow the Holy Spirit t
control and fill us, to that extent we are no stronger than an unbeliever.

The verse I read was Ephesians 4:19, "Having lost all sensitivity, they have given themselves over
sensuality so as to indulge in every kind of impurity, with a continual lust for more." (niv)

It was that last line, "with a continual lust for more," that gave me pause. The end result of this mo
depravity, according to Paul, was a "continual lust for more." Did I show signs in my life of a "cont
lust for more?"

What a good question for all of us to ask ourselves. In this verse Paul gives us the progressive dec
that leads a person to ultimately living a life (consciously or unconsciously) consumed with a "con
lust for more."

As believers, we are seeking to live a holy life in an unholy world that is bent on our spiritual, mora
physical destruction. It would do us all

well to be aware of the following three step progression of failure so we can do everything possible
avoid inadvertently falling into its subtle clutches.

The First Step: Callousness - "lost all sensitivity"

There is an obvious fact about our human nature. Whatever becomes common becomes "invisible
Our culture offers abundant quantities of things and experiences that can and will numb our spiritu
sensitivities. If we allow ourselves to be injected with enough carnal Novocain, our spiritual sensiti
will eventually become so diminished that we will no longer even notice the evil, the crude, the gre
the violent, the selfish, the blasphemous – it will simply become invisible. We can all likely think of
numerous examples when we have seen this happen.

Many translations use the word "callousness" in this verse. Calluses come from excessive use of s
part of your body – hands, feet, fingers, etc. Once a callus has formed, the feeling in that area of y
body is gone.

There is a little song I sang as a child that cautions against becoming calloused. You may know it.
is entitled, "Oh be careful little eyes what you see…" The other verses tell our ears to be careful w
they hear, our hands what they do and our feet where they go.

Each time we expose ourselves to the godless things of this world we receive another shot of
Novocain. Each shot further numbs our spiritual sensitivity and the ability of the Holy Spirit to prote
us from the deadliness of what we are exposing ourselves to.

...s numbing affect of the things of this world is no better illustrated than in Jesus' assessment of the ...ievers in the church at Laodicea in Revelation 3:15-18, "I know your deeds, that you are neither cold ...r hot; I would that you were cold or hot. So because you are lukewarm, and neither hot nor cold, I ...spit you out of my mouth. Because you say, 'I am rich, and have become wealthy, and have need ...nothing,' and you do not know that you are wretched and miserable and poor and blind and naked. ...dvise you to buy from me gold refined by fire, that you may become rich, and white garments, that ...u may clothe yourself, and that the shame of your nakedness may not be revealed; and eye salve to ...oint your eyes, that you may see." (niv)

...hn Calvin said, "Prosperity inebriates men, so that they take delights in their own merits. Nothing is ...re dangerous than to be blinded by prosperity."

...ese believers had become so numbed by the things of this world that they were not even conscious ...the fact that they were spiritually "wretched and miserable and poor and blind and naked." How ...uld this have possibly happened? They allowed themselves slowly over time to become numb to ...eir own materialism to the point of blindness. Have we, like them, become numbed by the appeal of ...e world so that we too are unaware of our own spiritual blindness?

...e way to avoid this downward spiral is to do whatever we can to avoid being injected with the ...mbing Novocain of worldliness and materialism.

...e Second Step: An increasing indulgence in our physical appetites - "indulge"

...nce we are adequately and spiritually numbed we will find ourselves feeling free to participate in what ...hn McArthur describes as, "unbridled self–indulgence." As the conviction of the Spirit and the Word ...e now muffled or silenced altogether, we will become like the believer in James 1:22-24, "But be ...ers of the word, and not hearers only, deceiving yourselves. For if anyone is a hearer of the word ...d not a doer, he is like a man who looks intently at his natural face in a mirror. For he looks at himself ...d goes away and at once forgets what he was like." (esv) He is no longer inclined to respond. He is ...ther inclined to forget. The numbness has done its work.

...ow, sufficiently numbed to spiritual reality and truth, we can blindly pursue, partake of and participate ...the things of the world without any feeling of contradiction or conviction. We can indulge our fleshly ...petites with little or no restraint. We can do things, buy things, wear things, watch things, eat things, ...ink things and say things totally oblivious to our spiritual inconsistency and opposition to the ways of ...od. Satisfying our appetites/pleasures can easily become a major focus, if not the primary focus of ...ur lives.

Controlling Our Lifestyle - Additional Food for Thought/Home Study Material

The Third Step: Addiction - "a continual lust for more"

Whenever we think of an addict we normally picture some pathetic crack user lying unconscious some back alley somewhere or the haggard drunk staggering home at 2:00 AM after getting him thoroughly "wasted." We don't like to think of addicts as people in suits and dresses, living in nic homes, going to good churches, running successful businesses and known as good Christians. we most certainly don't want to think of an addict as the person who is wearing our clothes and living in our house and is a respected member of our church and our community.

If we would be completely honest with ourselves, we would all admit that we are quite prone to addictions. In fact, most of our lives seem to be spent continually trying to avoid one addictive extreme or another. Be it food, drink, money, possessions, gambling, entertainment, sex, power, fame…the list goes on and on. The only real difference between us is which of these addictive tendencies we personally struggle with.

We can know we are addicted to something when we just won't give it up, even when we want t The rich young ruler wouldn't give it up (Matthew 19:22). Agrippa wouldn't give it up (Acts 26:28) Judas wouldn't give it up (John 12:4-6). The Pharisees wouldn't give it up (John 9:24-29). And countless millions of others in this world (believers and unbelievers alike) won't give it up either. T challenge for each of us is to honestly assess what "it" is in our lives – what is our insatiable "lust more."

The chorus of Casting Crowns' song Slow Fade poetically expresses what Ephesians 4:19 is warning us to avoid.

It's a slow fade when you give yourself away

It's a slow fade when black and white
have turned to gray
Thoughts invade, choices are made, a price will be paid
When you give yourself away
People never crumble in a day…

The key to overcoming the traps of worldly addictions is to first do everything we can to stay awa from the "needles of worldly Novocain" that are anxiously waiting to inject their numbing influence us – hoping that after we have been fully anesthetized we will painlessly and naively wander deep into the darkness unaware that we are in the midst of a "slow fade."

...ng An Overcomer

...Word gives us four clear directives on how to successfully avoid the enticing and numbing affects of ...world as we journey on towards eternity.

Be alert: I Corinthians 16:13, "Keep your eyes open for spiritual danger; stand true to the Lord; act like men; be strong…" (tlb)

Be serious: I Peter 5:8, "Be sober-minded… Your adversary the devil prowls around like a roaring lion, seeking someone to devour." (esv)

Be content: Philippians 4:11-12, "for I have learned to be content in whatever circumstances I am. I know how to get along with humble means, and I also know how to live in prosperity…" (nasb)

Be Spirit-minded: Romans 8:5, "For those who live according to the flesh set their minds on the things of the flesh, but those who live according to the Spirit set their minds on the things of the spirit." (esv)

...do not want to ever forget I John 4:4, "You are from God…and have overcome them (the false spirits ...his world); because greater is He who is in you than he who is in the world." (esv)

...e stay alert, serious, content, and Spirit-minded, we will overcome. May it be so for all of us.

Controlling Our Lifestyle - Additional Food for Thought/Home Study Material

Food for Thought Questions

1. Ephesians 4:19 says, "Having lost all sensitivity, they have given themselves over to sensua so as to indulge in every kind of impurity, with a continual lust for more." Would you find yourself struggling with a continual lust for more of anything?

_____

_____

_____

_____

2. What needles of worldly Novocain do you allow to numb your spiritual sensitivities?

_____

_____

_____

_____

3. Have you personally seen the statement, "Whatever becomes common becomes 'invisible be true in your regular exposure to what is worldly or evil?

_____

_____

_____

_____

Controlling Our Time

What is Your Most Valuable Possession?

What is your most valuable possession? When you first read this question your mind may quickly scroll through the list of all your possessions, looking for your asset with the highest value. For most people, you hear their home is their most valuable asset. For those whose net worth is larger, that is seldom the case. Instead, is it might be their business, one of their real estate holdings, or their investment portfolio? No matter which asset you may select as the most valuable, you will have picked the wrong one. Our materialistic culture drives us to think of our things when we think of our valuables, but there are other non-material things that are worth much more.

I would suggest to you that the correct answer to this question can be found by looking on a different balance sheet. Many years ago I heard Bob Buford, a self-made multimillionaire and author of the book Halftime: Changing your Game Plan from Success to Significance, speak at a conference. Right in the middle of the presentation he made a comment that was so profound and struck me so deeply that I could not think I really heard anything else he said for the rest of his presentation. He paused, gave a reflective look, and then commented, "It seems insane to me that a person would be willing to trade what he has a shortage of—time—in order to gain more of what he already has a surplus of—wealth." You cannot read this once and fully absorb it, so look at it again. "It seems insane to me that a person would be willing to trade what he has a shortage of—time—in order to gain more of what he already has a surplus of—wealth."

So, what is your most valuable asset? It is the time that you still have "banked" in this life. Your "time on this earth" account is all too quickly shrinking with every day that passes. And the most troubling part of this time account is that we cannot see how much we have left. Is it days, months, years, decades?

We often hear people ask the question, "How do you spend your time…?" This is a very accurate way to phrase how we use our time: we spend it. Unlike your financial accounts that you can make additional deposits into and build the account in the future, you can make no additional deposits into your time account. The total number of days allotted to us was deposited into our time account before we were even conceived. King David confirms this in Psalm 139:16, when he acknowledges, "And in Your book were written all the days that were ordained for me, when as yet there was not one of them." So, all of us will spend our time on something—and once it is spent, it is gone.

The truth of Bob Buford's comment is nowhere more clearly illustrated than in the story of the rich farmer we looked at earlier. After another excessive bumper crop season, he says,

> *This is what I will do: I will tear down my barns and build larger ones, and there I will store all my grain and my goods. And I will say to my soul, 'Soul, you have many goods laid up for many years to come; take your ease, eat, drink and be merry.' But God said to him, 'You fool! This very night your soul is required of you; and now who will own what you have prepared?'*
>
> Luke 12:18

ow pathetically sad. He was willing to trade what he had almost nothing left of—time—in order to gain ore of what he already had a surplus of—wealth. And then to add insult to his folly, God goes on to say of s man, "So is the man who stores up treasure for himself, and is not rich toward God" (Luke 12:21). He d not die rich—he died broke.

Psalm 90:12, Moses asks God to help him use his time account wisely. He prays, "So teach us to imber our days, that we may present to You a heart of wisdom." Paul said it this way in Ephesians 5:15-, "Therefore be careful how you walk, not as unwise men but as wise, making the most of your time, cause the days are evil." And not only are the days "evil," they are also very limited.

seems to me that we need to manage our time account with even greater care than we manage our vestment accounts. And we should be very leery about making any withdrawals out of our limited ne account—"spending our time"—in order to make additional deposits into our temporal, investment counts or even worse wasting our time on things that really don't matter.

ave consistently heard from many Christian families their honest acknowledgment that they have more oney to give than they have time. It is considerably easier for these believers to make a gift from their aterial possessions than it is to make a gift from their over-used and ever shrinking time account.

ep this in mind: it is not in how much of our stuff we give; it is in how much of ourselves we give that ows us to fully experience the joy and blessing of giving. As a nation, we have far too much material osperity to experience much real sacrificial giving, regardless of how much or how little of it we personally ossess. But we all have precious little to give from our time account, but this is where we, who are rich by e world's standard, learn to give like those who have little – by any standard.

ore and more families are catching the vision and seeing the power of short-term, family mission trips to edy countries. Can you guess what proves to be the greatest obstacle in pulling off such a trip? It is not pically the cost. That is frankly the easiest part of the trip. The hardest part of the trip is finding the time r all of the members of the family to make such a trip—to make a difference. The problem is the time, not e money.

hen I was a young boy, I spent a good bit of time visiting my grandmother. She was a zealous and ommitted Christian woman and everywhere you turned in her small home, there were signs of her faith—a ble on the coffee table—plaques and pictures on the walls—Bible verses on the refrigerator. There was e plaque in particular that made a significant impact on my thinking as a young boy. I did not realize then, but I do now. The little plaque read, "Only one life 'twill soon be past, only what's done for Christ ill last." Because of that compelling thought, my entire life, for the most part, has been one continuous tempt to use the brief time that God has allotted me to do something that will matter for eternity. Without is ultimate, eternal objective as our singular focus, life is correctly summed up by Solomon, "All of it is eaningless, a chasing after the wind" (Ecclesiastes 2:17 niv).

hat is your most valuable asset? How are you using your most valuable asset to do something that will st for eternity? Our cry should be, to paraphrase Isaiah 6:8, "Here I am Lord, [spend] me"

Controlling Our Time

Life Application Questions

1. What is your initial reaction to this video?

    _____

    _____

    _____

    _____

2. How did Bob Buford's comment… "It seems insane to me that a person would be willing to tra
    what he has a shortage of—time—in order to gain more of what he already has a surplus of—
    wealth" strike you? Are you guilty of being "insane"?

    _____

    _____

    _____

    _____

3. Why is the story of the rich farmer such a perfect example of what Bob is saying?

    This is what I will do: I will tear down my barns and build larger ones, and there I will store a
    my grain and my goods. And I will say to my soul, 'Soul, you have many goods laid up for r
    years to come; take your ease, eat, drink and be merry.' But God said to him, 'You fool! Thr
    very night your soul is required of you; and now who will own what you have prepared?'

    Luke 12:18-20

    _____

    _____

    _____

    _____

4. Are you like most affluent, American families who have more money to give than they do time?

    If this is true, then what is your most valuable possession? What are you doing to preserve and
    spend wisely this most precious of all possessions?

    _____

    _____

    _____

    _____

5. How do you respond to the comment, "It is not in how much of our wealth we give; it is in how much of ourselves we give that allows us to fully experience the joy and blessing of giving"? How do you respond to that idea? Do you get more joy out of writing a check or getting personally involved? Why?

_____

_____

_____

_____

6. The plaque mentioned read, "Only one life 'twill soon be past. Only what's done for Christ will last." What could you do with your limited remaining time on earth to accomplish something with your life that will last for eternity?

_____

_____

_____

_____

7. Moses tells us to "number our days that we may present to You a heart of wisdom" (Psalm 90:12). How many days do you have left if you live to your actuarial life expectancy?

Life Expectancy Using the RP-2000 Combined Healthy Mortality Table Projected to 2011																																															
Age	18	19	20	21	22	23	24	25	26	27	28	29	30	31	32	33	34	35	36	37	38	39	40	41	42	43	44	45	46	47	48	49	50	51	52	53	54	55	56	57	58	59	60	61	62	63	64
Male	62	61	60	59	58	57	56	55	54	53	52	51	50	49	48	47	46	45	44	43	42	41	40	39	38	37	37	36	35	34	33	32	31	30	29	28	27	26	25	24	23	23	22	21	20	19	18
Female	65	64	63	62	61	60	59	58	57	56	55	54	53	52	51	50	49	48	47	46	45	44	43	42	41	40	39	38	37	36	35	34	33	32	31	31	30	29	28	27	26	25	24	23	22	22	21

Age	65	66	67	68	69	70	71	72	73	74	75	76	77	78	79	80	81	82	83	84	85	86	87	88	89	90	91	92	93	94	95	96	97	98	99	100	101	102	103	104	105	106	107	108	109	110
Male	18	17	16	15	14	14	13	12	12	11	10	10	9	9	8	7	7	6	6	6	5	5	4	4	3	3	3	3	2	2	2	2	2	2	2	2	2	1	1	1	1	1				
Female	20	19	18	17	17	16	15	15	14	13	12	12	11	11	10	9	9	8	8	7	7	6	6	5	5	5	4	4	4	4	3	3	3	3	3	3	3	3	3	2	2	2	2	2	2	2

(Keep in mind, half of us will live longer and half of us will die sooner than these figures.)

What if you were to learn that you only had 30 days left on this earth? How would your life and the use of your remaining days change? What does this tell you about your real life priorities and how wisely you have used the time already spent?

_____

_____

_____

_____

Controlling Our Time

8. If you continue on the course your life is on right now, when you finally exhaust your "time account," how will you measure up to Ephesians 5:15-16, "Therefore be careful how you walk not as unwise men but as wise, making the most of your time…"? Have you made the most your time? If not, what would have to change for the answer to be, "Yes"?

    _____
    _____
    _____
    _____

9. Would you be willing to pray to the Lord, "Here I am, Lord, spend me?" What might happen i sincerely began praying that prayer on a daily basis?

    _____
    _____
    _____
    _____

IN CHARGE HERE?

Controlling Our Bodies

Housekeeping Matters

Many of you have likely attended a conference where someone gets up at the beginning of the conference to go over important housekeeping matters you need to know. Housekeeping matters are often important minor details that will help the conference run more smoothly – like hotel checkout time, restroom locations, scheduled break times, airport shuttle departures and so on.

However, I would like to suggest an alternate understanding of the phrase, that being "it matters how we keep our house" – in other words housekeeping really matters. The house I am suggesting that we need to be keeping is not the one made of wood and bricks that contains our stuff, but is the one made of flesh and blood that houses us and the Holy Spirit.

Paul tells us in I Corinthians 3:16, "Do you not know that you are God's temple and that God's Spirit dwells in you?" Notice our body is God's temple and as such we need to treat it as our mutual dwelling place.

There are three important reasons why it really does matter how well we are keeping our house.

First: Housekeeping Matters <u>Because it is Commanded</u>

I often hear people make off-handed comments suggesting that God isn't all that concerned about what we eat or how well we take care of our bodies – because, after all, we are going to get a new, perfect one later.

They will often quote Romans 14:14 where Paul assesses food in general, "I know and am persuaded in the Lord Jesus that nothing is unclean in itself…" They conclude that anything that can be chewed up and swallowed is acceptable fare for consumption and God really doesn't care what we consume.

Regarding exercise I hear frequently mentioned I Timothy 4:8 where Paul says, "for bodily discipline is only of little profit, but godliness is profitable for all things…" They conclude that because spiritual exercise is of greater value than physical exercise, physical exercise is unimportant.

But as caretakers of bodies that do not belong to us, I would like to suggest that we consider a broad perspective on the feeding and exercise of the bodies that God has entrusted to us.

Most believers are quite familiar with I Peter 1:15-16 which says, "but as He who called you is holy, you also be holy in all your conduct, since it is written, 'You shall be holy, for I am holy.'" Few realize that this is actually a quote from the Old Testament. And it may surprise you to know the context of where this phrase "be holy for I am holy" comes from.

In Leviticus 11:44-45 God is giving dietary directions to the children of Israel, "For I am the Lord your God. Consecrate yourselves therefore, and be holy, for I am holy. You shall not defile yourselves with any swarming thing that crawls on the ground. For I am the Lord who brought you up out of the land of Egypt to be your God. You shall therefore be holy, for I am holy."

This concept of being holy for I am holy comes right out of the middle of a chapter where God is telling His children what to eat and what not to eat. Keep in mind the word "holy" also means "pure." Apparently God does not want his children to defile the houses He has given them by consuming things that will physically defile (pollute/abuse) those physical houses.

We must understand that how we feed our house is not a means to spiritual approval. Paul points this out in I Corinthians 8:8, "Food will not commend us to God. We are no worse off (spiritually) if we do not eat, and no better off (spiritually) if we do." How we keep our house will have no affect on us after we leave this life. However, it can and will have a massive and often long-term affect on us while we are still in this life.

In spite of his comment, Paul still understood the need for strict physical discipline and the tragic, spiritual ramifications for failing to maintain such discipline. In I Corinthians 9:27 he says, "but I discipline my body and make it my slave, so that, after I have preached to others, I myself will not be disqualified."

What we eat and drink and how much we eat and drink has continually been an important physical issue with considerable spiritual ramifications for many centuries. It was as far back as the 4th century when the church first listed gluttony as one of the seven deadly/cardinal sins.

Physical housekeeping really does matter.

Second: Housekeeping Matters **Because it is Worship**

Paul gives us a second perspective on the extent that housekeeping matters when he challenges us in Romans 12:1, "Therefore I urge you, brethren, by the mercies of God, to present your bodies a living and holy sacrifice, acceptable to God, which is your spiritual service of worship."

Paul makes this same point in answering his own rhetorical question in I Corinthians 6:19-20, "Do you not know that your body is a temple of the Holy Spirit who is in you, whom you have from God, and that you are not your own? For you have been bought with a price: therefore glorify God in your body." We are to be glorifying God with and in our bodies.

In both these passages Paul connects our physical and spiritual lives together. He tells us that how well we keep our house should glorify Him and be an outward, physical expression of our worship of Him.

Is how you keep your body an act of worship for you? Does the current condition of your house bring Him glory? Is your housekeeping a clear demonstration of your loving and careful management of the dwelling place He has entrusted to you?

Physical housekeeping really does matter.

Controlling Our Bodies

Third: Housekeeping Matters <u>Because it is Smart</u>

Even if God hadn't commanded us to take good care of our houses and even if He hadn't told us that we worship Him by what we do with our bodies, there is still a third entirely pragmatic reason to take good care of our bodies that should itself be a compelling enough reason to be responsible housekeepers.

It has been my observation over the years that any asset left unmanaged becomes a liability. I have found no exception to this maxim whether it be materials things, relationships or businesses. You name it. If you buy a new car and never service the car, your asset will eventually turn into a liability. Likewise if you do not properly "service" your body, it will eventually become a liability too – sooner than it should.

The Center for Disease Control's report on the health of Americans is staggering. It estimates that of the 300 million Americans, 63% are considered overweight or obese; 80% of Americans over 25 are overweight; 78% of American's are not even meeting basic activity level recommendations.

According to former U.S. Surgeon General, Dr. C. Everett Koop of the 2.4 million deaths that occur in the United States each year, 75% are the result of avoidable nutritional factor diseases. In other words, 75% of Americans are suffering and ultimately dying prematurely from self-inflicted degenerative diseases due to the poor care and feeding of their houses.

Can you imagine the hundreds of millions of dollars of God's money God's people are needlessly spending on drugs, surgeries and healthcare to attempt to recover from the physical maladies that they have brought upon themselves by failing to make good long term lifestyle decisions? God's asset has been turned into a liability.

It is just smart to do whatever we possibly can to allow our houses to retain their vigor, their health and their vitality as long as possible. Because of the curse of Adam, all of our bodies are going to eventually wear out and cease to operate. But doesn't it make sense to postpone that time as long as possible by taking good care of our houses so they remain an asset that God can use for His purposes and His glory? The more healthy we remain, the more useful we can be for God's Kingdom and for His purposes.

If you knew that the next car you bought was going to be the last car you would ever own; if you knew that it was going to have to last for decades and even though there are some replacement parts available, you were going to have to live with whatever condition it was in, would you care for your car differently? I would. How much more should we treat our most valuable physical asset with meticulous care? This is the only body we are going to get this side of glory.

If you would like to develop a healthier lifestyle – become a better housekeeper, I would suggest you start with the book, *The Maker's Diet* by Jordon Rubin and then go from there. And don't forget the Owner's Manual. You would be absolutely amazed at what God has told us in His Manual about health, disease, diet, exercise, etc.

I hope as you pray and seek the mind of the Lord on this important but often ignored area of stewardship that you will come to agree with me that housekeeping matters.

Life Application Questions

1. What is your initial reaction to this video?

    _____

    _____

    _____

    _____

2. I Corinthians 3:16 says, "Do you not know that you are God's temple and that God's Spirit dwells in you?" What excuses or justifications have you made in the past to not care for the temple that God has entrusted to you?

    _____

    _____

    _____

    _____

3. I Corinthians 6:19-20 tells us, "Do you not know that your body is a temple of the Holy Spirit who is in you, whom you have from God, and that you are not your own? For you have been bought with a price: therefore glorify God in your body." How are you doing in glorifying God in your body?

    _____

    _____

    _____

    _____

4. Have you ever noticed how being in good shape physically actually helps you to be in better shape spiritually? If so, in what ways?

    _____

    _____

    _____

    _____

Controlling Our Bodies

5. Have you ever participated in an extended fast (more than 24 hours)? Why do you think the physical and spiritual exercise of fasting has been virtually abandoned by Christians today?

    _____

    _____

    _____

    _____

6. Romans 12:1 says you need to be "presenting your bodies as living sacrifices... of worship." Have you ever thought that how you feed and care for your body is actually a form of worship? Does that give you greater or lesser motivation to take better care of your body?

    _____

    _____

    _____

    _____

7. Is our relationship to Christ affected by our care and feeding of the temple that He has entrusted to us? Is our salvation at stake if we do not take good care of our body? If not, then, why should it matter how well you care for it? Isn't salvation all that really matters?

    _____

    _____

    _____

    _____

8. If you knew you were only going to get one car to drive for your entire life, would you care for it differently than you would if you knew you could trade it in on a new one in a few years? How, then, might we be more careful in how we care for our bodies if we were continually aware that this is the only one we get?

    _____

    _____

    _____

    _____

. What do the statistics mentioned from the Center of Disease Control tell about how well we are taking care of our bodies and our health? Why are they so ominous?

_____

_____

_____

_____

0. Should a follower of Jesus be more or less concerned about taking good care of his physical body than an unbeliever? Why or why not?

_____

_____

_____

_____

1. With all this new information on good housekeeping and its importance, what changes do you intend to make to do a better job of caring for His temple?

_____

_____

_____

_____

Giving Regularly

Giving Generously or Living Generously?

For many years I have been actively promoting the idea of generous giving. have written books and articles about it; I have taught on it; and I have help affluent families do it. To say the least, generosity is for me both a calling an a passion. But quite recently, the Lord has shown me through a sequence of unrelated events that I still have a lot to learn about what it means to be generous. Let me tell you the stories.

Recently on Sunday morning, at the end of our worship time, the worship minister announced that we were about to watch an extraordinary video about a couple in our church. As the video rolls, I an surprised – I know the husband, B.J. because I have played basketball with him at church for the pa few years. I liked him from the very first time we played ball together. B.J. is a young man in his late 20s, has a successful money management practice and is an extremely talented athlete. Since I kne one of the main characters in this video, I proudly nudged my wife and said, "I know him!"

My excitement turned to embarrassment as he and his wife shared their story. B.J.'s wife had a high school friend who was very ill and in need of a kidney transplant. Both of them immediately said to themselves, "Maybe we could give her one of our kidneys." Well, it seemed reasonable to me that B.J.'s wife might want to give her good friend one of her kidneys, but as it turned out B.J.'s kidney v the perfect match. So without hesitation he donated one of his kidneys to his wife's high school frier They shared that it just seemed like the right thing to do. B.J. had an extra kidney and this girl had none.

I was stunned. I wouldn't give one of my kidneys to one of my wife's friends. I would not even consic it. Of course I would give one to my wife or one of my children if they needed it, but to one of my wif friends? Don't get me wrong, I am all about giving of my time, talent and treasure, but giving my tors – my body parts? That was a level of giving that entirely surpassed my current concept of generosity.

Just a few days later, I was ready to board a plane to return home from a business trip. I was first in line and was looking forward to getting comfortable in my first class seat and then "zoning out" on th flight home. (I often get upgraded for free.)

Just prior to our boarding, a very heavy, crippled man had been escorted down the jetway in his wheelchair to board the plane. So I waited patiently for the call for first class to board. However, just they began to announce the first class boarding, another guy cuts right in front of me and hands the attendant his boarding pass. His rude manner and obviously arrogant attitude irritated me.

As we got to the bottom of the jetway, four airline staff were having difficulty getting the heavy, cripple man out of his wheelchair and into the airline wheelchair needed to get him on the plane. This delay was causing a back up in the jetway. No one was able to board because they were right in front of the plane door. So here I am standing and stewing over this rude guy who cut in front of me while I was waiting to get on the plane. I stood there a little impatiently watching the airline employees working futilely to get this crippled man into the airline wheelchair.

Then, the bomb fell. The guy who cut in front of me calls out to the flight crew, "Hey, let me help you." So he drops his bags and hurries over to them and helps get the man into the plane wheelchair. I was so ashamed. I was standing there just like the line-cutter was, but the thought never even crossed my mind to offer any help. Of all the people standing there watching this happen, this guy who I was convinced was so selfish and full of himself was the one who volunteered to help.

Unfortunately, the humiliation wasn't over. When they finally get the man in the wheelchair and through the plane door, Mr. Helpful then says to the airline staff. "Let me go back and get his bag for you." He comes back off the plane, grabs the man's bag, which by the way, is right at my feet and takes it back into the plane to him. Yet, another missed opportunity for me to live generously.

By this point I am feeling very convicted about my lack of generosity. Interestingly enough, it turns out the line-cutter is sitting right across the aisle from me in first class. I told him I appreciated his willingness to help the crippled man. He smiled and said, "It wasn't anything." To him, it wasn't anything, but to me it proved that of the two of us, I was the one who was selfish and full of myself, not him.

But God still wasn't finished rocking my generosity world. As I am finally relaxing in my first class aisle seat, the passengers in economy start filing past me. I hear a woman immediately behind me ask this soldier who is standing right next to me, "Soldier, what seat are you in?" He says, "21B." "One of the dreaded middle seats in the back," I thought. She then says to him, "Would you like to sit here?" The soldier hesitated, but the woman insisted that he take her first class seat and she would go back and sit in his middle economy seat.

Humbled again! This is all happening right next to me. Know that I deeply appreciate what our military does for us as a country and for me as one of its citizens. I have even thanked soldiers for their service on many occasions. But the thought of offering this soldier my first class seat and taking a middle seat in economy class on a packed plane was another indicator of just how limited my generosity really is.

I have been mulling these experiences over in my mind for a few weeks and I wanted to share with you the main lesson that I think God has taught me through this. The lesson is this: I can be generous in how I give without being generous in how I live. Conversely, I have also learned that a person who lives generously always gives generously.

In other words, we may be willing to be extremely generous in giving what we want to give where we want to give it. But with what we don't want to give we can actually find ourselves being just as selfish and tight-fisted as the infamous Ebenezer Scrooge. Living generously, not giving generously needs to be our goal.

I have identified three characteristics of people who model generous living:

Giving Regularly

Characteristic #1

Generous Living is Open-Hearted

Those who live generously are open-hearted and alert to find people who are struggling, hurting or pain. They empathize with those whose world is difficult and they enjoy trying to make it better.

Characteristic #2

Generous Living is Open-Minded

The minds of those who live generously are always thinking about creative ways to bless and encourage others in both great and small ways. They are consciously engaged in their world and t lives of those around them, poised to show generosity to anyone whenever the opportunity preser itself.

Characteristic #3

Generous Living is Open-Handed

The resources of those who live generously, all of them – (time, talent, treasure [and torso]), are ready to be gladly given whenever a need or an opportunity is discovered. When it is within their power to respond, they relish the privilege to make a difference and bless the life of another – frienc or stranger. They live out the extreme attitude, "What is mine is yours and you can have it."

In these three recent experiences it has been vividly demonstrated to me that the key to living a generous life is easy to understand. It is, however, excruciatingly difficult to live because of what it requires of us – a radical change in our self-assessment. Paul tells us in Philippians 2:3, "…but with humility of mind let each of you regard one another as more important than himself." There it is – in just one part of one verse – "regard one another as more important than himself."

If we can wholly embrace this radical change in our self-assessment – and truly come to believe that others are more important than ourselves, we will be completely transformed into not just people who are giving generously, but more importantly into people who are living generously – whe reflect an open-hearted, open-minded and open-handed life. If we really want to achieve maximum Kingdom impact in our lives, may I suggest that we expand our focus to not just giving generously, but more importantly to living generously.

Life Application Questions

1. What is your initial reaction to this video?

   _____

   _____

   _____

   _____

2. Which of the three stories shared were you able to most relate to and why?

   _____

   _____

   _____

   _____

3. Have you ever found yourself in a similar situation? What was it?

   _____

   _____

   _____

   _____

4. Why is it so much more difficult to live generously than it is to give generously?

   _____

   _____

   _____

   _____

5. Three characteristics were given of a person who lives generously.
   (1.) Open-Hearted   (2.) Open-Minded   (3.) Open-Handed

   Which of these is the easiest for you to live out and which is the most difficult?

   _____

   _____

   _____

   _____

Giving Regularly

6. Share some times in which you walked right past opportunities to be generous to someone because you were so distracted at the time with your own agenda that you missed the opportunities completely.

    _____

    _____

    _____

    _____

7. Discuss the quote, "I can be generous in how I give without being generous in how I live." How can we become more conscious about living generously so we can provide a more Christ-like example for the world to see?

    _____

    _____

    _____

    _____

8. Why is it important to keep Philippians 3:2 in the forefront of our minds in order to improve our efforts to become more overtly generous in how we live our daily lives?

    _____

    _____

    _____

    _____

Created to be Generous

Often times when we see or hear about people who are extraordinarily generous, we willingly credit them with having been given the gift of generosity. We know Paul's teaching. "We have different gifts, according to the grace given us. ...if it is contributing to the needs of others, let him give generously. (Romans 12:6, 8 niv). We point to that generous person and conclude that God obviously has given them the gift.

But in so acknowledging their gift of generosity we may actually be giving in to a very subtle deception that simultaneously excuses us for not being generous because we don't have the gift.

The Gift of Generosity

A gift, like the ones mentioned in Romans 12, are simply abilities that a person has been made natural better at something than he should be for the amount of time or effort he has put into it. You certainly know people who are gifted in certain areas like music, art, athletics, academics, public speaking, leadership, etc. What others have to work very hard at to become skilled, these gifted ones seem to do effortlessly. And when they exercise their gifts their skill levels go off the charts.

I am sure that some time in your life you have come across a youth that as soon as he touches a ball (pick your sport) for the first time, plays like he's been doing it for years; or the student, who never studies, yet gets straight A's; or the person who has never taken piano lessons, yet can play any music they hear; or the beginner who gets up to speak for the first time and communicates like an experienced orator. It is a gift from God.

Does this mean that the rest of us "ungifted" people can never learn how to play ball, the piano, get good grades, paint, skillfully speak, or lead others? I think not. What it does mean is that some people have been "super-charged" by the Holy Spirit with a gift and the rest of us mere mortals have to work hard to match the results these blessed ones are able to achieve so naturally.

We may see people who freely, abundantly, joyfully and even sacrificially give of themselves and what they have without any apparent reluctance, hesitation or fear. In comparison to their giving, ours is never as liberal or joyful. It is here that we can be deceived. We can mistakenly conclude that because we are not as good at giving as these gifted ones, we need not even try to imitate their example. If this is our thinking, we have come to the wrong conclusion.

Those that God has gifted with generosity are here to inspire and motivate us – to give us a glimpse of the incredible joy, impact and blessing that comes from being generous. God has given the gift of generosity to a few so they can serve as lighthouses to show the rest of us the way and to reassure us that it is not only safe to travel in that direction, it is absolutely the most exciting and fulfilling way to go. The generous ones are there to encourage us to follow the trail they have blazed!

My point is that generosity is not the exclusive domain of those gifted to be generous. Generosity is part of the hardwiring of every one of us. Let me explain.

Created in God's Image

Genesis 1:26-27 and 9:6 tell us that we have been created in God's image. We are in our very essence different than everything else that God created because we have the stamp of God's nature on us. And our goal in the Christian life is to allow ourselves to be "conformed into His image" (Romans 8:29) – for our image to match His.

We certainly can all agree that a dominate aspect of God's nature is that He is generous and this generosity flows out of His love. John 3:16 tells us, "For God so loved...He gave..." And this never-ending, unconditional love is demonstrated in His giving to us. "He who did not spare His own Son, but delivered Him over for us all, how will He not also with Him freely give us all things?" (Romans 8:32) Jesus said it this way in Matthew 7:11, "If you, then, though you are evil, know how to give good gifts to your children, how much more will your Father in heaven give good gifts to those who ask him!" Simply stated, our God is an extraordinarily generous God.

So, by the fact that we are created in God's image and God is a generous giver, we have all been created to be generous givers too!

Overcoming the Obstacles

Sadly, though, because of our fallen state we routinely smother our God-given generous nature. We cover it over with the lies of greed, self-interest, pride, fear and security. We often find ourselves so bedeviled by our obsession with ourselves that we routinely overlook the lives and needs of others around us. The still small voice of generosity within us – that invites us to ascend to a higher place – to a higher good – is tragically drowned out by the noise of our attention-consuming, selfish pursuits.

Paul, aware that selfishness is the core sin in our life that cripples, blinds and disables us from being conformed into the image of our loving and generous God, twice (Romans 12:3 and Philippians 3:2) instructs us to think of others as more important than ourselves. He knew that generosity towards others is the most effective antidote for the deadly disease of selfishness.

Yet, under this mountain of worldly and materialistic deception, like a smoldering coal buried under the ash of a dying fire, within every one of us, still remains a glowing ember that knows the most abundant, most fulfilled life is found not in what we have, but in what we give.

And if we will clear away the ashes of our "burned up" lives and give this ember of generosity some fresh air and new fuel, it will spark a blazing fire within us that will provide both light and warmth transforming us into what God has created us to be.

Giving Regularly - Additional Food for Thought/Home Study Material

We have all experienced even in our smallest, selfless acts of kindness to others – ("even a cup of cold water in my name…" [Matthew 10:42]) a heightened sense of aliveness, well-being and purpose when we bless the life of another in a meaningful way. Even in the simplest act of giving we find ourselves, albeit often briefly, connected to the heart of a generous God and in harmony with His divine nature. It is at this moment we are being conformed into the image of God and experiencing the joy of being like Him.

From our vantage point, people with the gift of generosity just seem to effortlessly "get it" and "do it." But for those of us who are not naturally gifted to be generous, we are still called to the same end – an extravagant life of generosity. Even though our path to a generous life will no doubt be much more challenging, fraught with many more obstacles, cluttered with many additional opportunities to "backslide" and demanding of us much greater spiritual, emotional and physical exercise to successfully ascend the same heights of generosity as those who have the gift, it is nonetheless the road we are all called to travel.

Most of us lack the gift of generosity, but all of us possess the nature of generosity. And it is this God-like nature of generosity that we must diligently cultivate and develop. And in so doing, the world will see the image of our generous Creator living and giving in us and we will, like the gifted, find "life indeed" (I Timothy 6:19 nasb).

Food for Thought Questions

1. How can we say that we want to be like God and Jesus without deeply desiring to be like them in generosity toward others (deserving or not)? (Remember, we were not deserving when God offered His generous salvation to us.)

_____

_____

_____

_____

2. Does being generous to others come naturally to you? If not, what can you do to cultivate your divinely generous nature in order to make you a more generous person?

_____

_____

_____

_____

3. How does our fallen, selfish nature prevent us from being as naturally generous as God created us to be? What can we do to rise above ourselves and make others more important than ourselves (Philippians 2:3).

_____

_____

_____

_____

Giving Regularly - Additional Food for Thought/Home Study Material

Generous Giver or Obedient Courier?

Over the past few years, I have become increasingly uncomfortable with the term generous giving. spite of that, I personally like the term. Both the words generous and giving are used in Scripture, a not in the same place very often (Psalm 37:21, James 1:5). However, as I continue to try to persona embrace and consistently apply the concept of biblical stewardship in my own thinking and life, the of the term generous giving has been creating in me more and more uneasiness. Here's why.

If someone labels a man a generous giver, it seems to imply two things about that man; (1) what he gives is his to give and (2) he decides how much to give [making him generous]. Within the context of biblical stewardship, however, both of these implications would be, at the least, misleading if not patently incorrect.

Let me make this point by asking you a question. Is it appropriate to describe a person as a generc giver if what he is giving is not his to give in the first place? Let me frame the question to be even m personal. "Would you describe a man as a generous giver if what he was giving away was, unknow you, coming out of your personal checking account and not his own?" I suspect you might have a descriptive terms for him, but generous giver would not be one of them.

Consider this hypothetical scenario. Imagine a very rich man decides to give his nephew $1,000,0C in cash. He calls his nephew and informs him that he is mailing him a certified letter with a cashier's check in it for $1,000,000 and the check will be arriving tomorrow. The next day the door bell rings there before the nephew stands the postman. The nephew can barely contain himself as the postm asks him to sign for the letter. The postman then hands the young man the envelope. The young m burst forward grabbing the postman in an enthusiastic embrace, gushing with thanks at how gener he is and how much the nephew appreciates his kindness for giving him such a generous gift. He repeats over and over again, "Thank you, thank you, thank you, you are just so generous!"

What is wrong with this picture? The truth is the postman did indeed give the nephew a cashier's check for $1,000,000. What is wrong is that the postman is getting all the acknowledgment and appreciation for making a gift that he merely delivered for someone else. He was in reality nothing n than the individual charged with the responsibility of delivering the gift to the proper person. I suspe the postman would have likely been quite surprised by the nephew's overflowing gratitude for simpl making a normal delivery as part of his routine duties.

Do you see my point? If we are merely stewards (managers) of our Master's property and not the owners, then nothing is ours to give away in any amount. And if our Master, the Owner, instructs us to deliver someone a gift from His abundance of which we are caretakers, then we are really being nothing more than obedient stewards commissioned to make the delivery to the designated recipie as instructed by the Owner.

When I was a young boy there was a television show called "The Millionaire" (1955-1960). For som reason that show had a significant impact on me as a child. In the series a very wealthy gentleman named John Beresford Tipton, Jr. would randomly give one million dollars, tax free, to people that were complete strangers to him. How Tipton delivered his cashier's checks was through his executive secretary, Michael Anthony. In each episode Anthony would deliver Tipton's check to a different individual. The rest of the show followed what happened to the recipient because of the gift. (It was almost always a bad outcome as I remember.) As he delivered the check, Anthony would make it quite clear that the gift was not coming from him, but from someone else who insisted on remaining anonymous. He was simply delivering the gift from this unknown benefactor.

It seems to me, this is the way it should be with us and our giving. We have been entrusted with assets for the purpose of delivering them to the intended recipient as per the directive of the Benefactor. When I watched "The Millionaire," I never thought of Anthony as being personally generous simply because he was the one delivering the checks. I only thought of him as doing his job – a fun job, no doubt.

Jesus describes this very idea in Luke 17:7-10 when he says, "Which of you, having a slave plowing or tending sheep, will say to him when he has come in from the field, 'Come immediately and sit down to eat'? But will he not say to him, 'Prepare something for me to eat, and properly clothe yourself and serve me while I eat and drink; and afterward you may eat and drink'? He does not thank the slave because he did the things which were commanded, does he? So you too, when you do all the things which are commanded you, say, 'We are unworthy slaves; we have done only that which we ought to have done.' " (nasb)

No matter how much we ultimately deliver of God's resources to the intended recipients, would the description of generous giver ever be appropriately applied to us because, "we have done only that which we ought to have done?" Maybe instead of using the term generous giver, it would be more appropriate to use the term obedient courier. This term, I believe, more accurately describes the proper stewardship mindset we should have in delivering generous gifts from the one and only Generous Giver.

In the Sermon on the Mount (Matthew 5:16), Jesus expresses this very idea when He says, "In the same way, let your light shine before others, so that they may see your good works (the delivery of the generous gifts) and give glory to your Father who is in heaven (the provider of the generous gifts)."

As we all seek to be good and faithful stewards, carefully and responsibly carrying out the delivery assignments of the Generous Giver, may we never lose sight of the fact that at most, "We are unworthy slaves;…having done only that which we ought to have done."

As we complete the remaining days of our life-journey, may each of us come to fully appreciate and joyfully embrace the sacred honor of humbly serving our Generous Benefactor as His obedient courier.

• 119

Giving Regularly - Additional Food for Thought/Home Study Material

Food for Thought Questions

1. How is understanding that God is the Owner of everything you possess change the way you should think about your giving?

   _____

   _____

   _____

   _____

2. Read Matthew 5:16, "In the same way, let your light shine before others, that they may see your good works (the delivery of the generous gifts) and give glory to your Father in heaven (Provider of the generous gifts)" (NASB).

   When you obediently deliver a gift from the Owner, what do you do to deflect the praise and gratitude for the gift to the Owner and not you as merely the courier?

   _____

   _____

   _____

   _____

3. How can remembering Luke 17:10, "We are unworthy slaves;…having done only that which ought to have done" help you keep a proper attitude about your part in the giving process?

   _____

   _____

   _____

   _____

121

IN CHARGE HERE?

Giving Regularly - Additional Food for Thought/Home Study Material

The Greatest Gift You Have to Give

Have you ever wondered why a poor, old woman living in the slums of Calcutta, India, who devoted her life to the mundane task of caring for unwanted, starving children was internationally known and revered and even awarded the distinguished Nobel Peace Prize? What did she do to deserve such impressive notoriety? Who was this woman? You and the rest of the world knew her. She was Mother Teresa.

By our materialistic, American standards, Mother Teresa was a miserable failure. She never owned her own home. She had no money set aside for retirement, had not built a successful business or had much of an income. She did not own a car and wore the same style of clothes every day.

There was no reason why this fragile woman living in the inner city of an obscure, economically struggling country, working with hundreds of seemingly insignificant children should have earned such worldwide respect and prestigious accolades.

The fact is that as a country, specifically, and as a world, generally, we have drifted quite far from our original moral, ethical, and religious moorings. However, we have not drifted so far from them that we do not still deeply respect people who are willing to sacrificially give of themselves to help the helpless. Deep down, each of us knows that in so doing we will experience the highest level of personal fulfillment and spiritual joy even though this reality is seldom part of our daily consciousness. Sadly, we often find ourselves so busy in our headlong pursuit of living life that we actually end up missing the true essence of life.

It is not enough to simply read the biographies of great men and women who throughout history have happily traded a life of prosperity, luxury, and comfort for one of toil, sacrifice, disease, and even death to help those who cannot help themselves. You may be inspired by their great religious and humanitarian efforts, but you will never experience their tremendous blessing. They would all acknowledge that the fulfillment they found surpassed everything they voluntarily gave up in the trade.

A group of twelve youth and adults traveled to Juarez, Mexico to build a home for a needy family.

The husband of the family, for whom the group was to build the home, worked sixty hours each week to earn $30. Their current home was a tiny, one-room shanty constructed out of shipping skids and wrapped in tar paper. Their three-year-old daughter was an invalid and had major respiratory problems. She could only go outside for a few minutes at a time.

The campsite where the group pitched their tents was an old cow pasture located across the road from a pigpen. The restrooms were pit toilets where it seemed half the flies in all of Mexico resided. If the flies did not drive you out, the smell would. The other half of the flies in Mexico swarmed over their food as they tried to eat. They slept on the ground, and from about 2 am on they were serenaded by a chorus of roosters making a sound night's sleep impossible. They cleaned up each day by pouring buckets of water over their heads. It was a challenging week for this group in many ways.

Yet, in spite of all of this, the group seized the challenge of building a humble dwelling for this needy family with the unity and zeal you might expect only from those who were building a grand palace for a king.

On the second day, as the team enthusiastically raised the walls to the new home, the mother stood by crying. All who saw her wept too. At that moment the group was reminded that they were not just building a house, they were helping people.

Seeing that woman's tears of joy made enduring all the discomfort of the trip wholly inconsequential. The group had again come to appreciate the words of Jesus, "It is more blessed to give than to receive" (Acts 20:35b). In this very small act of kindness, they had been reminded of this enduring truth.

What is interesting is that this group came home richer than they were before the trip. Some left their wives and children to go. Some took a week off work. They all spent money to go and they all endured physical discomfort. Yet, they came home richer. How? The answer cannot be explained in physical terms because it transcends the realm of the physical. It can only be explained in spiritual terms. And the explanation is this: You will always make a profit, when you give yourself away to others.

Let me suggest that the personal delight of giving massive sums of money away is decidedly minuscule in comparison to the joy you will realize by giving yourself away to a worthy cause.

The story of the rich young ruler expresses this truth perfectly. Jesus was not really interested in this young man's wealth. In fact, Jesus told him to give it all away to the poor. What Jesus really wanted was the young man himself.

What is the greatest charitable gift you have to give? Yourself! Why not make a gift of yourself to a worthy Kingdom cause? You will be all the richer for it.

Giving Regularly - Additional Food for Thought/Home Study Material

Food for Thought Questions

1. How have you personally given of yourself for the good of others?

   _____
   _____
   _____
   _____

2. What would have to change in your life to enable you to give more of yourself to others on regular basis?

   _____
   _____
   _____
   _____

3. If your life continues as it is now, what will people remember you for after you eternally reloc

   _____
   _____
   _____
   _____

Tithing: The Enemy of Generosity[1]

The idea of tithing as the standard for acceptable giving has so permeated the church that very few (including pastors and elders) even question its validity or application to those of us who are living this side of the cross. Many pastors and preachers emphasize tithing in hopes that their congrega will increase their giving above the national average of evangelicals, which is only about three perc They believe that if they could get everyone in their congregation to start tithing, the church would more money than it needed in order to do all that it wanted to do.

Consequently, pastors fervently teach tithing as the floor at which every Christian ought to start the giving—the minimum entry point. I know of one church in my town that requires attendees to com to tithing in order to become members. Pastors are not really aware that while their efforts to prom tithing might increase giving for a few, it actually ends up doing more harm than good to everyone their congregation.

Let me illustrate. Take any congregation that is being consistently and regularly indoctrinated with tithing as the giving standard. Those who, for whatever reason—good or bad—are not able or willing to tithe are made to feel guilty that they are giving less than they "owe" God. So their giving accompanied with feelings of guilt because they are told they are "robbing God." (See Malachi 3:8

Then you have those who are tithing to the penny. If they get a paycheck for $3,125.60, they will write a check to the church for $312.56. They are content to give exactly what they have been taught God has prescribed for them to give. Their giving will only increase as their income increase (mathematically to the penny).

Then there are those rare few who have broken over the tithe standard taught by the church and a now giving over ten percent. They often look upon themselves with some sense of pride because are actually exceeding the required, minimum standard of giving.

Now let me ask you, which of these attitudes of giving is healthy—giving with guilt, giving legalistic to the penny, or giving with pride?

You see, as soon as you employ some mathematical formula to determine how much someone ought to be giving—to determine what God expects—you actually create spiritual, psychological, a emotional barriers to generous giving. We are all fallen, sinful creatures and consequently want to k what the "rules" are because we want to please God. How much church attendance, prayer time, scripture reading, giving, etc. will be enough to keep God happy with us? So, if we accept a formu for giving, we will use it as the predetermined acceptable standard and no longer feel any need to s out God's will for our personal giving.

1 Excepted from E. G. "Jay" Link, Spiritual Thoughts on Material Things: Thirty Days of Food for Thought (Xulon Press, Longwood, FL, 2009), pp. 61-65. For a comprehensive study on biblical tithing go to www.StewardshipMinistries.org an read "Will a Man Rob God?" (Malachi 3:8): A Study of Tithing in the Old and New Testament by Andreas Kostenberger ar David Croteau.

However, the New Testament never mentions tithing as the rule and standard for New Testament Christian giving—not even one verse. There is a very good reason for this. The New Testament calls Christians to give by faith (life) and not to give by law (death). (See Romans 8:2.) How much I decide to give of what the Lord has entrusted to me is just as intimately personal and individual as every other aspect of my Christian life.

To put this into perspective, let me ask:
- Has God prescribed how many minutes I must pray each day?
- Has He stipulated how many verses He expects me to read each week?
- Has He established how many people I am required to witness to each month?

The answer is an obvious "No" to all of them. God has prescribed none of these as His "acceptable standard" for being a "good Christian." Rather it is up to each of us individually to seek the Lord by faith and allow Him to direct us in how much of these activities we should be participating in.

Similarly, our giving is to be arrived at by careful, personal self-examination and seeking the Lord's direction in how much we should give as we evaluate this crucial area of financial stewardship. May I suggest that 2 Corinthians 9:7 gives us the Christian methodology for deciding how much we personally should be giving back to the Lord, not the scriptures of the Old Testament on tithing. Paul instructs, "Each man should give what he has decided in his heart to give" (niv). In other words, the amount of our giving proceeds from our heart, not from our calculator. Our giving is to grow out of a personal relationship with Christ and not merely a prescriptive formula arrived at mathematically.

I can tell you with certainty that a poor woman who chooses to sacrificially give $500 out of her meager $12,000 annual Social Security income is being substantially more generous than the businessman who is giving $50,000 of his $350,000 annual income, even though the woman is giving only four percent and the businessman is giving fourteen percent.

Occasionally, I have been asked by affluent people, "How much should we be giving?" They sense that ten percent is no longer the right percentage for them and they are looking for someone to give them the appropriate percentage. My answer is always the same, "That is a very important question. Unfortunately, you are asking it of the wrong person. You need to ask that question to the One who owns all your stuff."

Many pastors I have talked with about generosity vs. tithing express the same gnawing concern. They fear that if they tell their congregation they are not required to tithe, the church's weekly offerings will collapse. I disagree. If believers were properly taught and really came to understand and live out the idea of generous giving by faith instead of legalistic giving by math, I believe that Christians' giving would explode. It may not happen overnight, because the church will have to overcome years of bad

Giving Regularly - Additional Food for Thought/Home Study Material

teaching, but once people really understand they need to go to their knees to decide how much to give instead of their calculators, we will likely see another outbreak of generosity that might compare what the Israelites experienced in the construction of the Tabernacle. Their giving was so "over the Moses had to command them to stop giving. (See Exodus 35:20-36:7.)

I recently attended a meeting in which the speaker was enthusiastically telling about a financial adv who had a wealthy client selling a $1.5 million asset, and the advisor had asked him about tithing o the sale price to the Kingdom, which he ended up doing. What struck me as unfortunate in this sto is that the advisor did not ask his client if he personally needed any of the sale proceeds. Maybe he should have given one hundred percent of the sale proceeds to the Kingdom—and if not one hund percent, how much might God want to use of these funds for His purposes? Possibly an even mor challenging question for this client to ask himself would be, "How much of this $1.5 million would I to give away for the gift to be a real, sacrificial act of faith on my part?"

The first option—the tithe—is clean, mathematically simple and requires little thought. The second-generosity—is neither clean nor simple and requires genuine soul searching, faith testing and "wres with God." In our struggle to find an amount right for giving each week, we might find ourselves fee compelled to ask a similar question, "How much would I have to give to the Lord in order for my gi to be both generous and sacrificial?"

I hope you can see why I say that tithing is the enemy of generosity. If believers are ever going to become generous givers, we must first kill the legalistic, Old Testament doctrine of tithing and repla with the New Testament directive of 2 Corinthians 9:7.

I would be remiss not to mention the "rest of the story" of 2 Corinthians 9:7 as well. Paul concludes this verse by giving us the emotional outcome of giving generously by faith vs. giving legalistically by math. He says, "Each man should give what he has decided in his heart to give, not reluctantly or under compulsion, for God loves a cheerful giver" (niv). Giving legalistically according to a formula to often produces a reluctant giver who is giving out of compulsion. Giving generously by faith produc a cheerful giver who is giving out of overflowing joy. Paul says this giver is the one whom God loves personally opt for the latter. How about you?

od for Thought Questions

1. How do you determine how much you will give? Does being free of the law of tithing make you want to increase or decrease your current giving? Why is that?

   _____

   _____

   _____

   _____

2. Have you ever been motivated to give out of guilt or obligation? When and why?

   _____

   _____

   _____

   _____

3. How much joy do you really receive through your giving? Why is that?

   _____

   _____

   _____

   _____

Giving Freely

Are You Living Like a Bucket or a Pipe?

Are you living like a "bucket" or a "pipe"? This is a rather odd metaphorical question, is it not? Yet, it is only odd until you consider the purpose of a bucket and the purpose of a pipe. A bucket is designed to hold things (liqu dirt, etc.). A pipe is designed to convey things through it (fluids, gases, etc The bucket holds what it receives and the pipe transfers on what it receive So, in regards to the wealth that God has graciously entrusted to you, let r ask, "Are you living your life like a bucket or a pipe?" Are you holding on or passing on?

The Way of the Bucket

It is easy enough to live like a bucket and there are three reasons why we can indeed find ourselves living like a bucket.

#1: We can find ourselves living like a bucket when we ignore the ultimate end of all bucke

I saw a bumper sticker some time ago that read, "He who dies with the most toys wins." I thought, "What an accurate way to express the world's view of life and possessions." But it immediately occurred to me that yes, this is true if the game of life is all about accumulation, the sad tragedy is that he who dies with the most toys still dies and then someone else will g to play with all his toys.

David reminds us in Psalm 49:16-17 niv,

Do not be overawed when a man grows rich (when he has a big bucket and it is full), when splendor of his house increases; for he will take nothing with him when he dies, his splendor not descend with him.

God condemns the rich farmer we discussed previously for this very thing: "God said to him 'You fool! This very night your soul is required of you; and now who will own what you have prepared (what is left in your bucket)? So is the man who stores up treasure for himself (kept own bucket full), and is not rich toward God" (Luke 12:20-21).

What we keep in our bucket will eventually leak out, be stolen, taxed, evaporate, or spilled o when you "kick the bucket." This should give us reason to pause as we consider the folly of living life like a bucket.

#2: We can find ourselves living like a bucket when we bestow on ourselves "Most Important Person" status.

When what we want and need becomes the center of our attention, we will find ourselves living like a bucket. Jesus sternly warns us about the narcissistic attitude that we are the center of the universe. Again, the parable of the rich farmer is the classic example. The farmer was incredibly successful and had more than his current "bucket" could hold, so he chose to get rid of his smaller bucket and get a larger bucket so he could hold all the new stuff that he had accumulated. Jesus nails the selfishness of the farmer in Luke 12:15 when He warns, "Beware, and be on your guard against every form of greed; for not even when one has an abundance does his life consist of his possessions."

The farmer's bucket was full and overflowing and he was proud of it, but God was not proud of him.

#3: We can find ourselves living like a bucket when we embrace the belief that filling our bucket is the way to find real happiness.

John D. Rockefeller honestly admitted, "I have made many millions, but they have brought me no happiness." However, we still want to believe the lie that "happy is the man whose bucket is full."

Henry Ford confessed after becoming a multi-millionaire, "I was happier doing a mechanic's job." Yet we still want to believe that "happy is the man whose bucket is full."

Solomon—who was perhaps the richest man to have ever lived—agonized about the futility of his riches in Ecclesiastes 2:11, "When I surveyed all that my hands had done and what I had toiled to achieve, everything was meaningless, a chasing after the wind; nothing was gained under the sun" (niv). But we still want to believe that "happy is the man whose bucket is full."

Solomon observed in Ecclesiastes 5:13 what happens when people try to keep what is in their bucket for their own selfish enjoyment, "I have seen a grievous evil under the sun: wealth hoarded to the harm of the owner" (niv).

Giving Freely

The Way of the Pipe

I think we can agree that even though our sinful, fallen nature entices us to live life like we are a buc
it is a cruel fantasy that ultimately leads to disappointment, destruction, and death. But what about
living like a pipe? Let us consider this alternative.

**#1: We will find ourselves living like a pipe when we understand God created us to be a pi
and not a bucket.**

In God's economy, a pipe is infinitely more useful to Him than a bucket! He created us to be
conduits and not receptacles of His blessings. In fact, let me ask you, "What happens if a
pipe gets confused and starts thinking it is a bucket?" What is supposed to pass through ge
stuck, becoming clogged and in need of being roto-rooted—so it can go back to doing wha
was made to do—which is to let things flow through it, not just to it.

Do you know what happens to the body when its arteries get clogged up? Or, what a proble
it is for the body when your colon gets clogged up? When your internal plumbing is not
working, your body is going to be greatly hindered in its normal activities.

God has created many of us to be high-capacity pipes because he wants to pump huge
amounts through us to support Kingdom causes worldwide. Let us look at what Paul tells
Timothy in 1 Timothy 6:17-19,

*Instruct those who are rich in this present world (high capacity pipes) not to be conceited or
fix their hope on the uncertainty of riches, but on God, who richly supplies us with all things
enjoy. Instruct them to do good, to be rich in good works, to be generous and ready to shar
(let it flow freely), storing up for themselves the treasure of a good foundation for the future,
that they may take hold of that which is life indeed.*

Nothing produces "life indeed" like doing what God has created us to do. God has positione
us to turn on our spigot and let it flow!

As R. G. Letourneau said when asked how he could be giving ninety percent of his income
away each year and yet still be getting richer. He smiled and confessed. "I keep shoveling it
and God keeps shoveling it right back in—and He has a bigger shovel!"

**#2: We will find ourselves living like a pipe when we really believe that what we are letting
flow through us today will ultimately flow back to us later.**

This is the great eternal "payback" for being a pipe. The bucket gets what it gets while it is h
and that is its reward. But the pipe receives a different payback. All that has flowed through i
for all those years of life are being recorded and it will all be waiting for us when we relocate t
our permanent residence. Malachi 3:16 says, "A book of remembrance was written before H
for those who fear the Lord and who esteem His name." God is monitoring your out-flow.

Jesus assures us of this eternal "payback" in multiple places. In Matthew 6:20-21, He encourages us, "But store up for yourselves treasures in heaven, where neither moth nor rust destroys, and where thieves do not break in or steal; for where your treasure is, there your heart will be also." We lay up for ourselves treasures in heaven by what we willingly divest ourselves of in giving to others in this life.

And again as we saw in Matthew 19:21, Jesus charged the rich, young ruler, "If you wish to be complete, go and sell your possessions and give to the poor, and you will have treasure in heaven; and come, follow Me." Pass it through now and it will be waiting for you in heaven. Jesus was not asking him to give it up; he was just asking him to send it on ahead for later use and enjoyment. Not a bad deal if we keep in mind that this life may last eighty years and eternity, well, it is a lot longer than that!

#3: We will find ourselves living like a pipe when the desires of God's heart truly become the desires of our heart.

Psalm 37:4 is a very powerful verse, "Delight yourself in the Lord; And He will give you the desires of your heart."

Most people have incorrectly interpreted this verse to say, "You delight yourself in the Lord and then the Lord will give you what you want," but it more accurately should be understood this way: "Delight yourself in the Lord and then the Lord will give you His desires for your heart." In other words, as we delight ourselves in Him, He will replace our heart's desires with His heart's desires, so that we will love what He loves and we will hate what He hates. That way we will have compassion on whom He has compassion.

And once God has our heart's desires aligned with His heart's desires, we will find ourselves driven to be a high-capacity pipe allowing as much grace and blessing as possible to fall upon those whom the Lord wants to touch and care for.

We must not forget the sobering words of our Lord who said, "From everyone who has been given much (high-flow capacity), much (high-flow capacity) will be required" (Luke 12:48b).

Jim Elliot, who was martyred trying to share Christ with a native tribe in South America, wrote, "He is no fool who gives what he cannot keep, to gain what he cannot lose." What we accumulate on this earth we cannot keep and what we accumulate in heaven we cannot lose. Seems like a "no brainer," does it not?

May I encourage those of you who God has blessed to be high-capacity pipes to freely open your spigot and let God's blessings and provision pour forth on those who need a blessing from God! If we do, we will have everything to gain and nothing to lose.

Giving Freely

Life Application Questions

1. What is your initial reaction to this video?

   _____
   _____
   _____
   _____

2. When you reflect on how you are currently living your life, do you see more similarities to living like a bucket or living like a pipe?

   _____
   _____
   _____
   _____

3. What are the three reasons given for why we might find ourselves living like a bucket?

   1. _____

   2. _____

   3. _____

4. Which of these three motivations do you most struggle with and how does it show up in your life?

   _____
   _____
   _____
   _____

5. Why do so many of us believe that more money for ourselves will make us happier in spite of all the horror stories of the devastation that money wreaks on those who possess it? Why do we so often choose to believe that lie?

   _____
   _____
   _____
   _____

6. What is your greatest struggle with the idea of consistently living like a pipe instead of a bucket?

   _____
   _____
   _____
   _____

7. "From everyone who has been given much (high-flow capacity), much (high-flow capacity) will be required" (Luke 12:48b). As affluent Americans, what should this verse be calling for us to do with our affluence, regardless of how much of it we have?

_____

_____

_____

_____

8. Do you think it would be exciting to live like R.G. Letourneau? Why or why not? What would prevent you from living like that, beginning today?

_____

_____

_____

_____

9. Psalm 37:4 says, "Delight yourself in the Lord; And He will give you the desires of your heart." Why is this verse so important to understand what David was really saying?

_____

_____

_____

_____

10. In what ways might there be an inconsistency between what Jim Elliott said, "He is no fool who gives what he cannot keep, to gain what he cannot lose" and how you currently live your Christian life?

_____

_____

_____

_____

11. In Matthew 19:21, Jesus charged the rich, young ruler, "If you wish to be complete, go and sell your possessions and give to the poor, and you will have treasure in heaven; and come, follow Me." Was Jesus asking him to give up his wealth or just postpone his enjoyment of that wealth until later? Why is this so important for us to keep in mind?

_____

_____

_____

_____

Giving Freely - Additional Food for Thought/Home Study Material

How Does the Love of God Abide in Him?

Do you have a verse or two in the Bible that you rather wish was not in there? I think all of us do. Like, maybe, "love your enemies" (Matthew 5:44) or forgiving people "seventy times seven" (Matthew 18:22) or "regard one another as more important than yourselves" (Philippians 2:3)? These verses like spiritual "thorns in the flesh" that continue to expose our lingering sinful, fleshly natures.

But there is another verse in the Bible that I also wish was not in there. And I expect when I share with you, you might wish it gone too.

In the movie The Wizard of Oz, Dorothy, Scarecrow, Lion, and Tin Man are cowering before the Wizard. Dorothy's dog Toto runs over to a curtain and pulls it back exposing a mere man pretending to be the great and powerful wizard. Do you remember what this man said to all of them as they stood there staring at him in shock? Still trying to perpetuate the fraud, still acting the part of the Wizard, he yells out over the loud speaker, "Ignore that man behind the curtain!" Well, after reading this verse, it will be very difficult to "ignore the man behind the curtain." The jig will be up. The real will be exposed. And if you are like me, when the curtain is pulled back, you will not at all like what others will see.

This troubling passage is found in 1 John 3:17 and it says (are you ready?), "But whoever has the world's goods, and sees his brother in need and closes his heart against him, how does the love of God abide in him?" Ouch!

"Whoever..."—Does whoever include me? Whoever?

"has the world's goods..."—Any goods? Does He mean surplus goods that I do not need or want—goods that if I gave them away would not affect my lifestyle? Or does this include worldly goods that I like and want to keep?

"and sees his brother..." —Any brother? Living anywhere in the world?

"in need..."—Any material need? Like hunger? Or thirst? Or nakedness? Or sickness? Or persecution?

"and closes his heart against him..."—You mean if I refuse to do something about his need?

"how does the love of God abide in him?"—Are you asking how does the love of God abide me?

Do you mean that unless I use my material possessions to meet people's needs when I am aware them, John is calling my love of God into question? I think it does. Ouch—no, double ouch!

Does this mean whenever I walk by a homeless person, I am supposed to respond to that need? What about when I see or hear about believers in other parts of the world who are suffering terribly? Is the love of God supposed to move me to do something about it with the worldly possessions I have at my disposal? When I hear about an orphan boy in Haiti who needs food, are you saying if the love of God is abiding in me, I will send him the $15 a month he needs?

Jesus said it this way,

> "For I was hungry, and you gave Me something to eat; I was thirsty, and you gave Me something to drink; I was a stranger, and you invited Me in; naked, and you clothed Me; I was sick, and you visited Me; I was in prison, and you came to Me." Then the righteous will answer Him, "Lord, when did we see You hungry, and feed You, or thirsty, and give You something to drink? And when did we see You a stranger, and invite You in, or naked, and clothe You? When did we see You sick, or in prison, and come to You?" The King will answer and say to them, "Truly I say to you, to the extent that you did it to one of these brothers of Mine, even the least of them, you did it to Me."
>
> Matthew 25:35-40

Do you mean in a very real sense when I look into the face of a suffering and needy believer I am looking into the face of Christ? And if I were to help that needy person using my worldly goods, I am actually giving to Jesus? Proverbs 19:17 says, "He who is kind to the poor lends to the Lord" (niv).

James 1:27 says, "Pure and undefiled religion in the sight of our God and Father is this: to visit orphans and widows in their distress." "Pure religion" is helping the helpless in their time of need. James goes on to ask in James 2:15-16, "If a brother or sister is without clothing and in need of daily food, and one of you says to them, 'Go in peace, be warmed and be filled,' and yet you do not give them what is necessary for their body, what use is that?"

Or still echoing in the background is John's piercing question, "But whoever has the world's goods, and sees his brother in need and closes his heart against him, how does the love of God abide in him?"

Is closing your heart against the poor as easy for you as it is for me? Are you able to see a need and in a matter of seconds, feel compassion and then almost instantly dismiss it with thoughts like, "Well, it is probably their own fault that they are in this mess anyway. They need to learn the hard lesson that God wants to teach them."

Or, "If I helped them out with some money, they would probably just use it for alcohol or drugs, but not for food. That would not be a good use of God's money."

Or, "The needs in that country are so massive that my little bit of money will not really make any difference—so why give anything?"

Giving Freely - Additional Food for Thought/Home Study Material

Or, my personal inclination, just look the other way and ignore them. The feelings of sadness and pity for the plight of the needy that might lead me to actually do something about their need, I have learned, will pass quite quickly if I just ignore them.

A family I know had allocated to each member of the family a certain sum of money to be used to meet the need of someone whose path they cross. As they were discussing what and how the he was going to be given, one of them spoke up and said, "You know just in the few minutes we have been discussing this, I have already come up with several ways to help." Other family members chimed in that they were thinking of ways to give too. Once you have a mindset that I have money to help and I want to get involved in making a difference in someone's life that has a need, the need and the opportunities seem to appear at every turn.

What has changed? Were these needs not there before this meeting? No, the needs were there. What was not there was the mindset that, "I am here on this earth to help those in need and I have some money set aside to do it with." It is a heart change that all of us need. For some of us with substantial wealth, we may need major heart surgery to extract ourselves from our tight grip on our possessions so that they can be used to impact the lives of people whom God has put in our path and graciously given us the funds to help.

Just try it. Allocate a certain sum of money—for example $1,000—and give yourself sixty days to and meet the need of a person or people who the Lord brings into your life. You will learn a few thi with this little exercise. One, God will show you more needs than your $1,000 can meet. Two, you will be personally and deeply impacted by seeing the results in the lives of those who have been th beneficiaries of your kindness and generosity. Three, you will want to do it again. It is addictive! Sta small and as God softens your heart and loosens your grip on your worldly possessions, your givir and need meeting efforts as well as your enthusiasm to give will grow.

After completing this giving exercise, get your Bible back out and re-read 1 John 3:17, "But whoe has the world's goods, and sees his brother in need and closes his heart against him, how does th love of God abide in him?" You will find that this verse no longer convicts and haunts you. It only affirms you and confirms your love for God. Now you can say, "I have the world's goods and I am constantly opening my heart and my hands to help my brothers in need and in so doing the love o God is manifested in my acts of love and kindness to those in need!"

If we have a surplus and know people who have a shortfall—and everyone that is hearing me does when we start giving to meet those needs we will rejoice over the words of 1 John 3:17 instead of feeling condemned by them. And that is a much better way to feel about the Word of God and a much better way to live.

Food for Thought Questions

1. When was the last time you spontaneously gave money to someone who you saw in need?

   _____

   _____

   _____

   _____

2. If you had money specifically set aside to meet the needs of the poor, how might it change your attitude about helping the poor when you do see them?

   _____

   _____

   _____

   _____

3. Based upon 1 John 3:17, are you willing to make helping the poor a priority in your life and your giving?

   _____

   _____

   _____

   _____

The Deeper Meaning of Life

If I were to quote the saying, "It is more blessed to give than to receive," would you know who originally said it or where it can be found? It might come as a surprise to you to learn that this statement was made by Jesus. However, it is found in a very unusual place. Whenever you think the statements of Jesus you immediately think of the Gospels and possibly His few comments in the book of Revelation. But this statement is actually found in the book of Acts 20:35. Paul quot it in his farewell address to the elders at the church of Ephesus after his three-year ministry with them.

What is particularly interesting about this is that Paul tells the elders to "remember the words of the Lord Jesus . . . Himself" suggesting that these words must have been widely known among believers even though they are not recorded in any of the Gospels. The Apostle John does tell u in the last verse of his Gospel, "Jesus did many other things as well. If every one of them were written down, I suppose that even the whole world would not have room for the books that wou be written" (John 21:25 niv). So, needless to say, there is much more that Jesus said and did tha is recorded in the Bible.

With that as a background, let us consider the verse itself. This verse is just another example of the idea of human contradictions. Jesus was a master of these. He would tell people if they wanted to be first, they would have to be last. If they wanted to live, they would have to die. If th wanted to be rich, they would have to become poor. This is just another in a long list. And this contradiction is nowhere more obvious than at Christmastime when giving and receiving reaches its annual apex.

Just ask a small child whether it is more fun—"blessed"—to get presents at Christmas or to give presents at Christmas, and the answer will always be the same. In fact, they may even look at you with some degree of disbelief. How could you even be asking such a ridiculous question? What keeps young children up at night with excitement is what they are going to get the next morning not what they are going to be giving. There is nothing wrong with a child who is almost delirious with excitement about what he will receive—it is very natural. And that is exactly my point. It is very natural. And Jesus is the master of calling us to the unnatural—like loving your enemies and forgiving those who hurt you.

Almost everything about being a follower of Jesus is unnatural or counterintuitive. In fact, it is a safe rule to follow that however you are naturally inclined to respond to a situation, respond just the opposite, and you will probably be responding the right way. You see, the spiritual dichotomy between what is natural and what is supernatural—which is how we have been re-born to live. T natural man will say, "It is more blessed to receive than to give." The supernatural man will say, " is more blessed to give than to receive."

we were completely honest with ourselves, we would all admit that it is a blessing to both receive and give. Notice, Jesus said, "It is more blessed to give than to receive." When the blessing of receiving overrides the blessing of giving, life becomes warped, myopic, and egocentric.

The story of Ebenezer Scrooge is a classic example of the natural man turned into the supernatural man. Ebenezer's life was consumed with getting and accumulating, while giving was an entirely foreign notion to him. In fact, it could be said he found the idea abhorrent to such an extent that when he was once asked to support the poor so they would not starve to death, he said, "Let them die and decrease the surplus population."

He would squeeze every penny out of every business deal he could, continuing to pile up greater and greater wealth. Yet, his receiving of more and more wealth failed to give him what he was looking for which was true happiness or fulfillment in life. In fact, the more he acquired, the more miserable he became. Something was terribly wrong with this lonely, old man. And the deceitfulness of believing that receiving was the greatest joy had failed him completely. He was not happy. He had no friends. He had no joy.

But then that one fateful Christmas Eve, Scrooge is forced to face himself through three spirits who visit him, and he becomes broken and changed. I mean totally changed—in just one night. How that change manifested itself was in an immediate transformation of his understanding of the purpose for all his accumulated wealth. He now saw it as a resource to be used for doing good. For the first time in his life he gladly opened his hands to help others as quickly and generously as he could. In all his giving he discovered the one truth that had completely eluded him all the years of his life—that it is more blessed to give than to receive.

Now this stingy, odious, crabby, hardhearted old man is changed into a generous, pleasant, kind and caring gentleman who finally found tremendous satisfaction in life—no longer in receiving and accumulating wealth for himself, but in giving that wealth in ways that would change people's lives and circumstances.

Sadly, King Solomon's life outcome was not as positive as Scrooge's. As one of the richest men who has ever lived on this planet, Solomon reflects back on all his material accomplishments in Ecclesiastes 12:1-11. Read it carefully.

I said to myself, "Come now, I will test you with pleasure. So enjoy yourself." And behold, it too was futility. I said of laughter, "It is madness," and of pleasure, "What does it accomplish?" I

explored with my mind how to stimulate my body with wine while my mind was guiding me wisely, and how to take hold of folly, until I could see what good there is for the sons of men to do under heaven the few years of their lives. I enlarged my works: I built houses for myself; I planted vineyards for myself; I made gardens and parks for myself and I planted in them all kinds of fruit trees; I made ponds of water for myself from which to irrigate a forest of growing trees. I bought male and female slaves and I had home born slaves. Also I possessed flocks and herds larger than all who preceded me in Jerusalem. Also, I collected for myself silver and gold and the treasure of kings and provinces. I provided for myself male and female singers and the pleasures of men—many concubines. Then I became great and increased more than all who preceded me in Jerusalem. My wisdom also stood by me. All that my eyes desired I did not refuse them. I did not withhold my heart from any pleasure, for my heart was pleased because of all my labor and this was my reward for all my labor. Thus I considered all my activities which my hands had done and the labor which I had exerted, and behold all was vanity and striving after wind and there was no profit under the sun.

I have always wondered if instead of doing all this stuff "for myself," if Solomon had done these things for others, would he have come to the same pessimistic conclusion about his life and his work? "All vanity and striving after the wind and there [is] no profit under the sun." I somehow think not.

With all of Solomon's wisdom, there is one truth that he sadly missed entirely, "It is more blessed to than to receive" (Acts 20:35).

Giving is a natural outgrowth of mature love. We see this so plainly in John 3:16, "For God so loved He gave…" And we can all be thankful that His desire to receive our gifts of worship and praise was exceeded by His desire to give us a gift that we could never buy for ourselves. Romans 6:23 reminds us that "the free gift of God is eternal life in Christ Jesus our Lord."

A biblical approach to life cannot focus simply on maximizing what you will keep for yourself and your family. You must also strive to address the deeper issues of your life's purpose—what can you do to maximize your blessing to others?

It is the introduction of this aspect of giving that brings purpose, meaning, and fulfillment into what would otherwise be nothing more than a set of difficult business decisions that need to be made in order to minimize the damage of taxes. It is this component that gives planning a heart. It is what gives it life.

If you want to experience the deepest meaning in life, let me encourage you to follow the converted Scrooge's example—and not Solomon's—in regards to your accumulated wealth.

Food for Thought Questions

1. Do you receive more joy when you get things or when you give things? What does this say about your level of spiritual maturity in understanding the deepest meaning of life?

   _____
   _____
   _____
   _____

2. How important of a role does giving to others play in your life?

   _____
   _____
   _____
   _____

3. If you asked ten people who know you well whether they saw you as being more of a giver or a taker, what would they say? Ask ten and find out.

   _____
   _____
   _____
   _____

• 143

Giving Freely - Additional Food for Thought/Home Study Material

Letting Your Left Hand Know What Your Right Hand is Doing

One of the most misunderstood passages in the Bible is found in Jesus' Sermon on the Mount where He discusses giving. Here is what He actually says.

> Matthew 6:1-4, "Beware of practicing your righteousness before other people in order to be seen by them, for then you will have no reward from your Father who is in heaven. Thus, when you give to the needy, sound no trumpet before you, as the hypocrites do in the synagogues and in the streets, that they may be praised by others. Truly, I say to you, they have received their reward. But when you give to the needy, do not let your left hand know what your right hand is doing, so that your giving may be in secret. And your Father who sees in secret will reward you."

A common misunderstanding of what Jesus is teaching here has led many believers to conclude that unless your giving is entirely anonymous, you will receive no reward from the Lord for your gifts. I once heard a gentleman who was sharing his giving testimony acknowledge that by sharing what he did, he would now be losing his reward. Some people have taken this misbelief about anonymous giving so seriously they only give cash to their church so as to make it impossible for anyone to trace their giving.

Is this what Jesus is teaching? I think not. In fact, I think we will have missed Jesus' point entirely if that is what we conclude. It is good to remember that chapters 5-7 are one sermon. We must not ignore the rest of what Jesus says. Context is key here. I think there are three important lessons about giving we can draw from Jesus' sermon.

He Teaches Us to Give

We must not overlook the obvious. Jesus tells us "when you give" – He does not say if you give. Giving is an expected and commanded part of being a follower of Jesus. His teaching here begins with the assumption that every follower of Jesus will be giving. He then addresses the dangers and pitfalls you must avoid when you do your giving.

I fear many immature and "non-giving" believers (and there are a huge number of them) use this passage as a way to not give and keep their non-giving a secret. If ever confronted with what they are giving, they can hide behind this passage that their giving is a secret. I once asked a church body this question, "Do you think if the giving records of each member of the church were to be posted on the bulletin board, anyone would be embarrassed by the other members knowing what their giving was. We never did it, of course, but it does point out how many believers will hide behind this teaching to cover up their lack of generosity.

He Teaches Us to Give <u>Purely</u>

The point that Jesus is really trying to make here is about our giving motives. He says that we should never do our giving, "in order to be seen by them" and subsequently to be "praised by others." In other words, we do not want to give because of what we might get from it – like others having elevated thoughts of us or making complimentary comments about us or us receiving some special treatment because of our giving. Jesus is saying that if your motive for giving is to draw attention to yourself and you accomplish that, you received the reward you wanted. It is not so important whether your giving is known by others, it is more important to know how and why your giving was made known to others.

If you study Jesus' entire sermon, you will see the progression of His message. In the last half of chapter five (verses 21-48), He emphasizes inner moral righteousness, providing us six specific illustrations of murder, adultery, divorce, oaths, revenge, and love. In the first eighteen verses of this sixth chapter He emphasizes outward formal righteousness and gives us three representative illustrations of typical religious activities – that being giving, praying and fasting. These three activities are all connected in the flow of His message.

It is important to understand this because Jesus also teaches us to go into our closet (6:6, KJV) to pray and not to do it publically. Isn't it interesting that we stringently believe our giving ought to be the ultimate private act, yet, we do not apply the secrecy doctrine to prayer even though Jesus' teaching on both of these practices are almost identical? He even adds one additional common religious practice of that day (one that might be good for us to revisit) when He tells us that your "fasting may not be seen by others but by your Father who is in secret. And your Father who sees in secret will reward you" (6:18).

Do you see the repetitiveness in each of these three illustrations? Do something with pure motives and do not seek to be seen and admired by others. Then God, who knows the true motives of your heart, will reward you in your giving, praying and fasting. Why do we put giving in a different category from the other two? Giving needs to be private, but we don't hesitate to ask people to audibly pray and be heard by others?

Let me also add that if anonymous giving is the only proper way to give, how is it that not only was Jesus able to watch people giving their offerings in Luke 21:1-4, He was so close to the offering box that He could actually see the amount the widow gave. He praises the amount of her gift (making it public) using it as a lesson to challenge His disciples and countless millions of believers through the ages. So much for anonymous giving. Jesus Himself blew her cover. Did she lose her reward because of it? I think not.

Additionally, if giving was meant to be a secret, why are we told about the many believers who gave in Acts 2:45 and also Barnabas and others who gave recorded in Acts 4:32- 37? All this was public knowledge and even recorded by Luke for all future believers to know about. You see, it is not about secrecy, it is about motive. We should be motivated to give as an act of personal worship and not so we might be praised and honored by others for what we have given. If that is the motive, then that person has "received [his] reward."

Giving Freely - Additional Food for Thought/Home Study Material

He Teaches Us to Give Purely <u>to Glorify God and Motivate Others</u>

Jesus' sermon also teaches us what the proper motivation for our giving and good works should be. In 5:6 Jesus says, "In the same way, let your light shine before others, so that they may see your good works and give glory to your Father who is in heaven."

If we keep our giving and good works under a bushel (5:15 – a secret) thinking this is what Jesus wants, how can we obey this part of His sermon? We are told here to let our light (our giving and good works) "shine before others so they may see your good works…" Taken at face value it seems that Jesus is contradicting Himself. We must understand that Jesus is addressing the giver's motive (i.e. to "give glory to your Father who is in heaven") and not who knows about the good gift. If in our giving and doing good we always seek to deflect the praise and glory for giving from ourselves (6:1-4) to God (5:16), acknowledging that, "every good thing given and every perfect gift is from above, coming down from the Father of lights…" (James 1:17), we are being obedient to both passages. If we readily seek to deflect the praise from our known giving to the Father, then we will always be safe from others ever thinking more highly of us than they should (Romans 12:3).

Let me also suggest a second healthy motivation for actually making your giving known. Hebrews 10:24 tells us, "…let us consider how to stimulate one another to love and good deeds…" I can think of no more compelling reason to make our giving known to others than in so doing to challenge other believers to step up their level of generosity and experience the joy and the blessing that comes from increased giving.

Just think how much poorer we would all be if the likes of J. C. Penny and R. G Letourneau who both gave away 90% of their massive incomes during their lifetimes would have never let us know what they were doing. Or, what about Stanley Tam (God Owns My Business) and Alan Barnhart who both have given their entire companies away to the Lord, choosing to live on modest salaries and funneling millions of dollars of company profits to Kingdom causes worldwide annually? What about all the Bible characters who fill the pages of Scripture who inspire and challenge us to greater levels of sacrificial giving? What if they would have all kept it a secret? What a loss for us!

So Jesus' message about giving is both clear and simple. 1. Give. 2. Give purely. 3. Give purely to glorify God and motivate others. Rather than concern yourself with who is aware of your giving, instead focus on who will be glorified by your giving and who you might inspire to join you in your giving adventures. So, if your motives are pure – go ahead and let your light shine before others, so that they may see your good works and give glory to your Father who is in heaven. The more who are blessed and inspired by your giving, the better!

Food for Thought Questions

1. Will this concept of anonymous giving affect the way you give? If yes, in what ways?

_____

_____

_____

_____

2. Have you ever used anonymous giving to "cover up" your lack of personal giving?

_____

_____

_____

_____

3. In what ways can you give to bring more honor to God and to motivate others to give more also?

_____

_____

_____

_____

Giving Extravagantly

When Giving Got Out of Control

If you want some excellent examples of generous giving, you need only look in the Bible itself. In two different passages we witness some extraordinary and compelling giving stories. One is in the Old Testament and the other is in the New Testament. One involved people who were rich, and the other involved people who were poor. One was for a building program and the other was for benevolent needs. Quite a contrast in many ways, but the outcome in both stories was identical – their giving got out of control.

In the first out-of-control story Moses has come down from Mt. Sinai, his face literally aglow, and reports to the children of Israel that God wants them to build a tabernacle for Him to dwell in. It is important to keep in mind that even though the Israelites were slaves in Egypt for centuries, when they did finally leave that country, they left incredibly wealthy. (See Exodus 12:35-36).

In the second out-of-control story the Macedonian Christians are in the midst of enduring both extended and extreme poverty – themselves barely surviving. Yet, they hear from Paul that the Christians in Jerusalem are facing even more desperate conditions than they are.

Here is Out-of-Control Story #1

(Exodus 35:20-36:7) Then all the congregation of the sons of Israel departed from Moses' presence. Everyone whose heart stirred him and everyone whose spirit moved him came and brought the Lord's contribution for the work of the tent of meeting and for all its service and for the holy garments.

Then all whose hearts moved them, both men and women, came and brought brooches and earrings and signet rings and bracelets, all articles of gold; so did every man who presented an offering of gold to the Lord. Every man, who had in his possession blue and purple and scarlet material and fine linen and goats' hair and rams' skins dyed red and porpoise skins, brought them.

Everyone who could make a contribution of silver and bronze brought the Lord's contribution; and every man who had in his possession acacia wood for any work of the service brought it. All the skilled women spun with their hands, and brought what they had spun, in blue and purple and scarlet material and in fine linen. All the women whose heart stirred with a skill spun the goats' hair.

The rulers brought the onyx stones and the stones for setting for the ephod and for the breastpiece; and the spice and the oil for the light and for the anointing oil and for the fragrant incense. The Israelites, all the men and women, whose heart moved them to bring material for all the work, which the Lord had commanded through Moses to be done, brought a freewill offering to the Lord.

Then Moses said to the sons of Israel, "See, the Lord has called by name Bezalel the son of Uri, the son of Hur, of the tribe of Judah. And He has filled him with the Spirit of God, in wisdom, in understanding and in knowledge and in all craftsmanship; to make designs for working in gold and in silver and in bronze, and in the cutting of stones for settings and in the carving of wood, so as to perform in every inventive work. He also has put in his heart to teach, both he and Oholiab, of the tribe of Dan. He has filled them with skill to perform every work of an engraver and of a designer and of an embroiderer, in blue and in purple and in scarlet material, and in fine linen, and of a weaver, as performers of every work and makers of designs."

Now (they) and every skillful person in whom the Lord has put skill and understanding to know how to perform all the work in the construction of the sanctuary, shall perform in accordance with all that the Lord has commanded. Then Moses called every skillful person in whom the Lord had put skill, everyone whose heart stirred him, to come to the work to perform it. They received from Moses all the contributions which the sons of Israel had brought to perform the work in the construction of the sanctuary.

And they still continued bringing to him freewill offerings every morning. And all the skillful men who were performing all the work of the sanctuary came, each from the work which he was performing, and they said to Moses, "The people are bringing much more than enough for the construction work which the Lord commanded us to perform."

Then Moses gave an order and they sent this word throughout the camp: "No man or woman is to make anything else as an offering for the sanctuary." And so the people were restrained from bringing more, because what they already had was more than enough to do all the work.

Here is Out-of-Control Story #2

(II Corinthians 8:1-5), "And now, brothers, we want you to know about the grace that God has given the Macedonian churches. Out of the most severe trial, their overflowing joy and their extreme poverty welled up in rich generosity. For I testify that they gave as much as they were able, and even beyond their ability. Entirely on their own, they urgently pleaded with us for the privilege of sharing in this service to the saints. And they did not do as we expected, but they gave themselves first to the Lord and then to us in keeping with God's will."

These two stories are extraordinary examples of what happens when God's people get out of control in their motivation to give. I think it would be quite instructive for us to go behind this explosion of generosity to determine what prompted this kind of out-of-control giving in these two circumstances. I have identified four lessons we can learn from these two stories.

Giving Extravagantly

Lesson #1:

Giving will get out of control when <u>God's people catch a bigger vision</u>

Both these visions for doing something greater than themselves began with strong leaders who had a clear vision and were able to effectively articulate that vision and the plan to achieve it – Moses had the blueprints for the tabernacle and Paul intended to personally deliver the benevolent support to the believers in Jerusalem.

I think Will Rogers understood the need for a good plan to accompany a good vision when he stated "A vision without a plan is a hallucination." Or, as the old proverb says, "A vision without a plan is just a dream. A plan without a vision is just drudgery. But a vision with a plan can change the world." Both leaders had a vision and a plan.

I have a friend who repeats often, "You're getting what you're getting because you're doing what you doing." In other words more of the same leads to more of the same. This is where most believers find themselves in their giving journeys.

In both these stories, God's people were challenged to embrace a vision that was substantially bigge and more challenging than anything they could envision themselves and they embraced the vision an exceeded all expectation in supporting it as a result.

Lesson #2:

Giving will get out of control when <u>God's people surrender themselves to the Lord</u>

The most obvious statement of this lesson is when Paul says that the Macedonians first gave themselves to the Lord. The beginning of any outbreak of generosity will begin when God's people surrender to Him.

I use the word surrender and not submit for good reason. To submit means to give in. We submit to the authorities over us (government, employers, husbands, etc.) not necessarily because we like wha they are doing or agree with their actions, but because we are commanded to submit – to give in – to respectfully yield.

Surrender, on the other hand, is to give up. In this case, there is no objection, no resistance, no biting our lip, no holding our tongue and reluctantly obeying. We completely surrender our will, our opinion, and our self-interests. This is what I believe Paul is getting at when he says that the Macedonians first gave themselves to the Lord. They gladly and willingly surrendered what little they had in material possessions to God. They surrendered their personal agenda for what they wanted to do with those possessions (like having another meal) to God's agenda of helping other believers who were even mo needy than they were.

When God's people finally and fully surrender (give up) to God instead of just submit (give in) to God of respect and duty, out-of-control giving will be positioned to happen.

Lesson #3:

Giving will get out of control when <u>God's people attune their hearts to the voice of the Holy Spirit</u>

We see this repeatedly mentioned in the story of the Israelites. It says the spirit moved them, their heart(s) were stirred and the people were filled with the spirit of God.

When God's people tune their "inner radio" to the right frequency – the frequency of God's voice instead of the frequency of this present age, an eruption of generosity is poised to happen.

Sadly, many pastors, ministers, and church leaders have guided their people to look at their calculators to determine their required level of giving instead of directing them to look to the Holy Spirit for His desired level of giving. The former inhibits out-of-control giving.

Paul is quite clear on the basis for Christian giving in II Corinthians 9:7 (just one chapter after his report of the Macedonian's out-of-control giving). He says, "Each one should do as God has purposed in his heart…" Here Paul is offering us a procedure for determining our giving and not a percentage for determining our giving. He is telling us to tune into the guidance of the Holy Spirit who can stir and move our hearts and fill us with an eagerness to give at levels far beyond anything we have experienced previously.

Lesson #4:

Giving will get out of control when <u>God's people experience joy in giving</u>

Both stories abound with comments about the extraordinary levels of joy His people experienced as their giving got out of control. They had overflowing joy. The people were bringing much more than enough. They were restrained from bringing more. They urgently pleaded for the privilege of sharing. They gave beyond their ability.

Wouldn't you love to be part of a worship service one day where the leaders of the church get up at the offering time and tell the congregation that they are not going to take up an offering because they already have more than enough to perform the work that the church is doing? It would be a modern day manifestation of out-of-control giving.

If you read the rest of II Corinthians 9:7 you will see this fourth lesson emphasized. Paul concludes his giving instructions that we should give, "…not grudgingly, nor under compulsion, for God loves a cheerful giver." The Greek word for "cheerful" could also be translated "hilarious." When the act of giving itself brings us out-of-control joy, out-of-control giving is on the verge of breaking out.

Giving Extravagantly

How can we increase our joy in giving? One way would be for when we give to actually be able to see the results of our giving – the lives that will be changed or the work that will be done. I have heard of surveys that indicate that of all the giving that Christians do, church giving gives them the least amount of joy. One reason is because the church has done such an inadequate job of connecting their members to the impact their weekly giving is having in the lives of people locally and internationally. Their giving simply goes in the plate, never to be seen or heard about again. Yet, these same folks derive great joy in supporting a needy child in a third-world country. Why? It is because they are connected to the recipient and to the outcome.

Wouldn't it be inspiring if each week just prior to the offering, your church would show a short one minute video of someone who has been impacted by the ministry of your church – a person who got saved – a marriage that was rescued – someone who was helped to overcome an addiction – a child who was impacted by a VBS program – a tribe in a foreign country that now has the Word of God in their language, etc. because of the ministry of the church? You could call this little video vignette the "Money Clip." Wouldn't that make giving more meaningful and much more joyous for everyone?

Connecting giving to specific outcomes opens the door for greatly increased joy in giving. And the more "hilarious" we become in our giving the more likely we are to start giving like the Israelites in Exodus 35-36 and the Macedonians in II Corinthians 8.

If you want to experience out-of-control giving, (1.) embrace a bigger vision, (2.) totally surrender to the Lord, (3.) listen to the Holy Spirit, and (4.) make your giving a joyous experience. Then, look out!

Life Application Questions

1. What impresses you the most about these two out-of-control giving stories?

_____

_____

_____

_____

2. Does the statement, "You're getting what you're getting because you keep doing what you're doing" apply to your giving and the blessings you are getting from it?

_____

_____

_____

_____

3. What is the biggest Kingdom vision you have ever been part of?

_____

_____

_____

_____

4. Why is the word *surrender* emphasized instead of the word *submit* when it comes to our obedience to Christ's will? Why is *surrender* a requirement of out-of-control giving?

_____

_____

_____

_____

Giving Extravagantly

5. II Corinthians 9:7 instructs us that "Each one must give as he has decided in his heart, not reluctantly or under compulsion, for God loves a cheerful giver." What make this New Testament directive for giving so revolutionary to the Old Testament concept of giving?

    _____
    _____
    _____
    _____

    Paul is giving us a procedure for giving instead of a percentage for giving. (Discuss this giving procedure and how we are to settle on how much to give.)

    Have you ever felt like you were being forced to give? Have you ever given grudgingly before? What is Paul telling us about that kind of giving?

    _____
    _____
    _____
    _____

    Of all the giving that you do, which of it brings you the least amount of joy and why? What can be done to make all our giving a *hilarious* experience?

    _____
    _____
    _____
    _____

6. What has been the most personally meaningful (joy-filled) gift you have ever made and why was it so?

    _____
    _____
    _____
    _____

7. If you were to (1.) start looking for a God-sized vision, (2.) surrender fully to the Lord, (3.) tune your heart to the voice of the Holy Spirit and (4.) find places to give that would bring you great joy, would your giving substantially increase? If yes, why? If no, why not?

    _____
    _____
    _____
    _____

Taking Hold of Life Indeed

I Timothy 6:17-19, as plainly as any place in scripture, makes it abundantly clear what those who possess surplus, material prosperity are to do with their prosperity and why. Here, the Apostle Paul instructs young Timothy:

> *Command those who are rich in this present world not to be arrogant nor to put their hope in wealth, which is so uncertain, but to put their hope in God, who richly provides us with everything for our enjoyment. Command them to do good, to be rich in good deeds, and to be generous and willing to share. In this way they will lay up treasure for themselves as a firm foundation for the coming age, (NIV) so that they may take hold of that which is life indeed. (NASB)*

Paul knows that the successful accumulation of wealth does not automatically make one spiritually wise, biblically learned, or even morally good. Consequently, these holders of substantial, material possessions require spiritual direction in addressing their circumstances just as much as those who are materially poor. The directives are different, but both are equally needed. Paul, in the strongest language – command them – directs Timothy in what the prosperous are to be doing with their prosperity.

Paul emphasizes three important points in his commands to those with surplus possessions.

#1 – Anchor Your Hope

Paul indicates that there are two places people can anchor their hope for this life and the next – either in the provided or in the Provider. You can place your hope in your stuff or you can place your hope in the One who provides you with the stuff (Deuteronomy 8:18). If your hope is in your possessions, you have anchored your hope to an uncertain security. Proverbs 23:5 warns, "Cast but a glance at riches, and they are gone, for they will surely sprout wings and fly off to the sky like an eagle." Putting your hope in your stuff is like putting your hope in the wings of a bird.

The words of a great old hymn says it best, "My hope is built on nothing less than Jesus' blood and righteousness…on Christ the solid rock I stand all other ground is sinking sand." As Jesus taught us in the Sermon on the Mount (Matthew 6:24), "No one can serve (put their hope in) two masters. Either he will hate the one and love the other, or he will be devoted to the one and despise the other. You cannot serve both God and Money."

Anchoring our hope in God leads us to humility. Anchoring our hope in our possessions leads to pride. And we know God hates pride. (Proverbs 6:16-17)

#2 – Share Your Abundance

The advantage of possessing material riches is that it enables its possessors to become rich in an additional way – in good deeds. In the same way they have been successful in accumulating their wealth, they are now being commanded to be successful in sharing their wealth to the point that they are seen as being generous. It is the privilege and the responsibility of the affluent to be so.

I have long appreciated the enduring truth of Proverbs 11:25,"…he who refreshes others will himself be refreshed." Generosity is never one-sided. The giver is refreshed by the giving as much as the receiver is refreshed by the receiving. It is a double blessing – both are refreshed in the act. In other words, "he who seeks to improve the lives of others will himself have his own life improved."

This truth is entirely counter-intuitive to our human nature, as is all of the Christian life. We discover that if we are hungry – and go feed someone else who is hungry, we will be filled. If we are cold – and give someone else our blanket who is cold, we will be warmed. If we are discouraged – and give someone else our attention who is discouraged, we will be encouraged. In the world's material economy, none of this makes any sense. But in God's spiritual economy, it is the way to finding life indeed. When we change our focus from inward to outward then the lights of heaven come on and brighten our day.

Paul knows that generosity is the antidote to the spiritually debilitating disease of "affluenza" which is so easily contracted in a materialistic culture like ours. That is why Jesus tells us that the way to avoid this dreaded disease is to "store up for yourselves treasures in heaven…" (Matthew 6:20) by sharing your surplus with those who have a short-fall. To disobey this command to be generous will result in what Solomon observed of the ungenerous affluent, "There is a grievous evil which I have seen under the sun: riches being hoarded by their owner to his hurt" (Ecclesiastes 5:13). It is really a very simple principle, "Share, you keep. Keep, you lose."

What may be the hardest part of this command is that Paul orders the affluent to not only be generous with their material wealth, but also to be generous with themselves – to be rich in good deeds. They are to be generously giving of themselves. It is not enough to just write a check to meet needs. Paul is commanding the wealthy to get personally involved in meeting needs.

Giving Extravagantly - Additional Food for Thought/Home Study Material

#3 – Enjoy Your Reward

Paul tells us that if we focus on converting our temporal, material wealth into eternal, spiritual wealth, we will find a great reward in this life and in the next. Jesus instructs us in Luke 16:9, "I tell you, use worldly wealth to gain friends for yourselves, so that when it is gone, you will be welcomed into eternal dwellings." By doing so, you are converting temporal, material wealth into eternal relationships. Jesus tells us that one day we will be separated from our wealth. So the wise man will invest that wealth while he has it to produce eternal relationships that he will be able to enjoy forever.

C. S. Lewis said it this way, "Aim at heaven, and you will get earth thrown in, aim at earth and you will get neither." Are we working to convert our temporal, material wealth into eternal, spiritual wealth? Paul tells us that by being generous, we are laying up treasures for [our]selves. Do we really believe what Paul is telling us? If we do, why would we not gladly and zealously obey this command to be generous?

Paul makes one final and powerful point regarding enjoying the reward for obedience. Our earthly generosity becomes the material with which God will lay a firm foundation for us in heaven. If we want a "mansion" in heaven, we need to be sending on ahead the needed materials (by our generosity in this life) so that the required construction materials will be available to lay the appropriate foundation.

What we keep or consume on ourselves in this life, stays in this life. What we share of what we have and who we are with others – what we generously give – we are sending on ahead for our heavenly enjoyment – forever. We are blessed by giving, others are blessed by receiving, and we are blessed again in glory with a reward that is proportionate to our earthly generosity. Talk about a win-win-win deal.

Our time on this planet can never fully provide us with life indeed. It is at best a cheap imitation of the real thing. As the old hillbilly would say, "Ya ain't seen nothin' yet!" The best is undoubtedly yet to come.

So, Paul is commanding affluent believers to #1 – Anchor your hope on the Rock: #2 – Share your abundance with others: #3 – Enjoy your reward of generosity in this life and in the next.

Remember I John 5:3, "This is love for God: to obey his commands. And his commands are not burdensome…" "Trust and obey. For there's no other way, to be happy in Jesus, but to trust and obey."

ood for Thought Questions

1. Why do you think most pastors and ministers are so hesitant to preach and teach boldly about our responsibility to give generously?

   _____

   _____

   _____

   _____

2. Why are we foolish to put our hope in our material possessions?

   _____

   _____

   _____

   _____

3. What have been the times in your life where you think you may have gotten more of a blessing out of your giving than the receiver? Why is that?

   _____

   _____

   _____

   _____

WHO'S IN CHARGE HERE?

Giving Extravagantly - Additional Food for Thought/Home Study Material

Big Giver/Small Giver: Someone Has Reversed the Definitions

One of the most radical giving passages in the entire New Testament is found in Luke 21:1-4. You most likely have heard the story about the "widow's mite." Most people completely miss how profound this story and Jesus' teaching on it is. In fact Jesus, as He did on many occasions on many different subjects, turns the Old Testament teaching on giving "on its ear" with His comment.

Here is the brief story. "Jesus looked up and saw the rich putting their gifts into the offering box, a he saw a poor widow put in two small copper coins. And he said, "'Truly, I tell you, this poor widow has put in more than all of them. For they all contributed out of their abundance, but she out of her poverty put in all she had to live on.'" (esv)

A person could all too easily read right through this story, be warmed by the sweetness of it and move on. But we dare not overlook the fact that in Jesus' assessment, He reverses our commonly understood definitions of what makes big giving big and what makes small giving small. He chang the entire paradigm by identifying the widow as the big giver and the wealthy as the small givers – this poor widow has put in more than all of them.

To fully appreciate the extreme contrast in Jesus' comparison here, we need to understand that these two small copper coins this poor widow gave was the equivalent of 1/64th of a common laborer's daily wage. Assuming a minimum wage for an eight hour day, her gift amounted to a measly ninety cents in today's dollars. Contrast this with the huge sums of money that Jesus observed the rich dropping into the offering box. Their giving may have even been bags of gold – surplus gold. And that is His point. Even the significant amounts of money the rich were parting with in their offerings would have absolutely no immediate or long term impact on their lives whatsoever. They were giving what they did not need and what they would not miss. In their giving they were making no personal sacrifice at all. The widow, on the other hand, would likely feel the impact of her gift by dinner time that very day.

Let me also note the percentage of giving Jesus endorsing here before we move on. You can chec my math, but I believe it is 100%, not just some arbitrary or perfunctory 10% tithe. He is praising and promoting 100% giving. That alone is "off the charts" extreme teaching.

A Modern Day Comparison

In order to better understand what Jesus is actually saying here, let me give you a hypothetical, modern day situation to illustrate the extent of just how radical this redefining of what big giving is. Imagine there are two members of your church. The first member is a poor, elderly widow who receives $12,000 a year in Social Security and who gives out of her meager annual income $500 a year to the church. The second member is a successful businessman who is giving $50,000 a year to the church from his $350,000 annual income?

Comparison #1

If you compare the total dollar amount the two are giving, who is the big giver and who is the small giver? Pretty obvious, the businessman is the big giver and the widow is the small giver. The businessman is giving 100 times more than the widow.

Comparison #2

If you compare their giving as a percentage of their income, you will see that the widow is giving a very modest 4% of her income – (an unacceptable amount in many churches' theology). The businessman on the other hand is giving a very healthy 14% of his income. If you compare the percentages of income the two are giving, the businessman is again the big giver and the widow is the small giver. The businessman is giving 3.5 times more.

Comparison #3

However, Jesus ignores our two "normal" methods of measuring the liberality of giving and instead institutes a brand new giving measurement never before used. Simply stated, here is Jesus' new definition for measuring generous giving: Your degree of generosity is not measured by how much you give, it is measured by how much you have left over after you give. This is such a profound truth you cannot hear this statement just once and fully absorb it, so let me give it to you again. Your degree of generosity is not measured by how much you give, it is measured by how much you have left over after you give.

Using Jesus' new definition to measure who is the bigger giver, we are not to compare their total giving (comparison #1) or even their percentage of giving (comparison #2), we are to compare how much the widow and the businessman have left over after they have made their respective gifts (comparison #3).

The widow has a meager $11,500 left over to live on for the entire year (less than $1,000 a month), while the businessman must "struggle" to make ends meet on his remaining $300,000 salary ($25,000 a month). The message is unmistakably clear here. Jesus' teaching, in this case, is telling us that the widow who gave only $500 is a much bigger giver than the businessman who liberally gave $50,000.

Jesus has thrown us an incredible curve in His comparison in Luke 21 when He identified the poor widow, not the rich, as the bigger giver.

Giving Extravagantly - Additional Food for Thought/Home Study Material

The Most Generous Person I Have Ever Personally Known

I have worked with many affluent families over the past 30 years and I have helped them make seve[r]
substantial gifts to the Kingdom. However, when I think about the most generous person I have eve[r]
known, none of these committed and willing givers reach the top of my list.

That top position goes to a ten-year-old boy named Jimmy Mitchell who was a member of my chur[ch]
back when I was preaching as a young man well over 30 years ago. One Sunday before church, I w[as]
standing up at the pulpit getting my sermon notes ready and Jimmy came running into the auditoriu[m]
of our very small country church in rural Kentucky. He ran up to me with a one dollar bill in his hand
and said, "Jay, look what I've got." I said, "Jimmy, that's great. Where did you get it?" He told me
that after he mowed his yard, he decided to go ahead and mow his elderly neighbor's yard next doo[r]
because she wasn't able to get around very well. He excitedly exclaimed, "After I finished, she came
out and gave me this dollar."

He then paused and gave me a reflective look and said, "You know, Jay, I'd like to give some of this
dollar to the Lord." Touched by his comment, I replied, "Jimmy, I know the Lord would be so please[d]
that you would want to share some of that dollar with Him. How much do you think you would like t[o]
give Him?"

Even after over three decades now, I still remember his penetrating words like it was yesterday. He
looked down at the dollar and then questioningly looked up at me and asked, "Do you think He wou[ld]
mind if I kept a dime?"

His words still ring in my mind to this day, "Do you think He would mind if I kept a dime?" Jimmy kne[w]
whose dollar it was and he was just hoping to enjoy some small benefit from it having passed throug[h]
his hands on its way back to its rightful Owner for His use and purposes.

Even after thirty years, Jimmy Mitchell still remains the most generous giver I have ever personally
known. Not because of the total amount of the gift – a meager 90 cents, or even the amazing
percentage of his giving – 90%, but because of the amount he had left over after he made the gift –
one thin dime.

I have never personally given this sacrificially and extravagantly at any time in my life. Have you? Can
you imagine what the Kingdom of God would look like today if it were full of believers who thought an[d]
acted like Jimmy Mitchell?

Your degree of generosity is not measured by how much you give, it is measured by how much you
have left over after you give. This new definition of what makes a person a big giver should challenge
all of us to reassess our current level of giving to determine if we should even be thinking of ourselves
as big givers.

It may just be that based upon Jesus' revolutionary, new definition of what it means to be a big giver,
some of us who may have previously thought of ourselves as big givers aren't all that big of givers
after all and many of us who likely have never thought of ourselves as big givers indeed really are!

Food for Thought Questions

1. How do you personally respond to Jesus' change in the definition of what makes a person a big giver? With these new definitions, have you become a bigger giver or a smaller giver?

   _____

   _____

   _____

   _____

2. What was it about the story of Jimmy Mitchell that made the biggest impression on you?

   _____

   _____

   _____

   _____

3. How will this teaching from Jesus on giving change how you think about your giving and how much you give going forward?

   _____

   _____

   _____

   _____

Well Done...

For Richer or For Poorer

We most often hear this phrase, "for richer or for poorer" in wedding vows, but I believe this phrase may also be used to describe a core issue for us in regards to our giving. Let me explain. I have observed over the years that one of the most compelling disincentives to people's giving is a nagging sense of loss from what they give away. Many feel that if they give, they will become "poorer" in the same proportion as the recipient of their gift becomes "richer." In other words, "Someone else's gain is at my expense." So, they think, "I need to evaluate how much I can afford to lose in my giving – how much poorer I am willing to become – in order to determine how much I am willing to give."

May I suggest that this kind of thinking, common as it is, is the absolute opposite of what the Word of God teaches us about giving. The Bible unquestionably teaches us that our giving is never a personal loss. It is always a personal gain. In fact, I hope to convince you that it is impossible for any of us to divest ourselves of our acquired wealth by giving it away to bless and serve others.

Let me begin by first asking you a simple question. When you put money into your retirement plan or make a principal payment on your home mortgage loan, do you feel poorer in so doing? I think not. We understand that we have simply transferred these funds to a different asset that is not immediately useful, but will ultimately be very beneficial to us in the future. I would go so far as to say that in making these transfers we actually feel better off financially and even more secure by doing so, even though our net worth statement has not changed at all in the transfer.

There is a repeated phrase in the New Testament that I believe most of us have not carefully considered. The phrase "Lay up treasure(s)" is used in Matthew 6:20, Luke 12:20 and I Timothy 6:19. It is interesting that the Greek word for "lay up" is related to the root word for "treasure." So, you could literally translate the phrase, "treasure up treasures." We read, for example, in Matthew 6:20 that we are to be "lay(ing) up treasures in heaven."

What seems to have escaped our notice is the two other words that are in the middle of this phrase - "for yourselves." Jesus says, "lay up treasures for yourselves in heaven." These treasures are not being laid up in heaven for God, or for the poor or for the lost. We are laying them up for ourselves. We are not losing them, we are simply transferring readily liquid and immediately available assets into an account that is not immediately liquid nor readily available, but will be of great value to us in the future. And every gift (transfer) we make in this life is being credited to our account in heaven – every one of them, no matter how great or how small.

In I Timothy 6:17-19, Paul reiterates this same idea when he is writing to Timothy about the affluent Christians under his spiritual care. He says, "Command those who are rich in this present world not to be arrogant nor to put their hope in wealth, which is so uncertain, but to put their hope in God, who richly provides us with everything for our enjoyment. Command them to do good, to be rich in good deeds, and to be generous and willing to share. In this way they will lay up treasure for themselves as a firm foundation for the coming age, so that they may take hold of that which is life indeed."

These affluent Christians are not being commanded to divest themselves of their material treasures, they are being commanded to lay up their treasures for themselves – for later enjoyment – "for the coming age" – an eternal retirement plan or equity position.

The rich farmer is called a "fool" in Luke 12:20 because he was mistakenly "laying up treasures for himself" here on earth. He was properly investing for himself, only he was doing it in an improper place! (See Matthew 6:19.)

Let me even go so far as to say that we cannot give anything away that we possess. We can at best only lay it up in a different account. But in the end, no matter where we give it, it has been credited to our heavenly balance sheet and it will make us ultimately (and sometimes even immediately) richer than before we made the transfer. Add to this fact that when we lay up (invest) treasures for ourselves in Kingdom things, God's return on that investment is always guaranteed - never a downturn in God's economy. Remember, investing in the Kingdom for the King always makes you richer – never poorer.

Let me give you just a few additional scriptures that further confirm the immediate and ultimate profitability of laying up treasures for yourselves in heavenly things.

We read in Acts 20:35, "In all things I have shown you that by working hard in this way we must help the weak and remember the words of the Lord Jesus, how he himself said, 'It is more blessed to give than to receive.'" We gain.

Proverbs 11:25 tells us, "A generous man will prosper; he who refreshes others will himself be refreshed." We gain.

In Luke 6:38, Jesus encourages us, "Give, and it will be given to you. A good measure, pressed down, shaken together and running over, will be poured into your lap. For with the measure you use, it will be measured to you." We gain.

• 165

Well Done...

We can see in these verses that we are not just richer financially, but also emotionally because our giving refreshes us as well as those we give to; spiritually because our giving more perfectly conform us into the image of Christ – the ultimate giver; and relationally because not only do we profit from ou investment, others profit as well – a double blessing.

I am reminded of the young boy who gave Jesus what was no doubt a hearty lunch of five loaves and two fishes (Matthew 14:13, Mark 6:33, Luke 9:12, John 6:1). (This story is one of a very few that is actually reported in all four gospels. It obviously made a huge impression on everyone.) I am confident when the boy gave his sack of food to Jesus he thought he was giving up his lunch – a los But he was okay with that. After all, it was for Jesus. Little did he know that not only would he still have his lunch, but thousands of others would also have lunch thanks to him. Having once been a young boy myself, I imagine this lad likely ended up eating more than his original five loaves and two fish before the day was done. He wasn't poorer because of his gift, he was actually richer and so we all those who were with him. No loss.

Anne Frank, the young Jewish girl who was eventually killed in a Nazi concentration camp wrote, "No one has ever become poor by giving." Do you know why? Because you cannot become poor by giving. It is an eternal impossibility.

Do you see yourself as being poorer after you write the check or make the gift? Do you feel like you have lost and someone else has gained? Do you sense that you are worse off than you were before you gave? Perish the thought! You are richer! You have just laid up for yourself more treasures in heaven. You are now more blessed and your future more secure than before. You have willingly transferred some readily available, immediately liquid assets to another account that will be waiting fo you when you finally "retire" from this life and move on to the next one – the best one. And in that day you will be glad you invested so generously with a long view of life and eternity. Someday, oh, happy day, all our invested treasures will finally be returned to us to use and to enjoy - forever!

Life Application Questions

1. What is your initial reaction to this video?

   _____

   _____

   _____

   _____

2. Do you find yourself feeling "poorer" after you give? Why is that?

   _____

   _____

   _____

   _____

3. Does this feeling of loss reduce the amount you might otherwise give? Why do we believe that in our giving – "the receiver's gain is at our loss?"

   _____

   _____

   _____

   _____

4. Read Matthew 6:20, Luke 12:21 and I Timothy 6:19 and check the context of the phrase "Lay up...treasures." Who are we supposed to be laying up treasures for? Why is this important for us to know and fully embrace?

   _____

   _____

   _____

   _____

Well Done...

5. Do you think it is wrong or that it cheapens the motive for our giving if we are rewarded for our giving? If yes, where have you come up with this idea?

    _____

    _____

    _____

    _____

6. Whose idea was it to reward us for our obedient deployment of the Owner's funds? Why is it important to know whose idea this is?

    _____

    _____

    _____

    _____

7. Discuss the statement, "We cannot give anything away that we possess." What does this mean? How is this possible? How can it be true?

    _____

    _____

    _____

    _____

8. Do you think the young boy who gave his lunch to Jesus thought he sacrificed his lunch that day so Jesus could eat? What do you think this boy must have thought after he saw what Jesus did with his lunch?

    _____

    _____

    _____

    _____

9. Where is the only place you can invest and have it be absolutely secure and with returns of up to 10,000%? (This is what "hundredfold" means. See Mark 10:30.)

_____

_____

_____

_____

10. Anne Frank said, "No one has ever become poor by giving." Why is it not possible to become poor by giving?

_____

_____

_____

_____

11. What do you think Jesus meant when He said, "It is MORE blessed to give than to receive?" (The giver is rewarded more than the receiver.)

_____

_____

_____

_____

12. How will this understanding of being rewarded for what we give of ourselves and the resources we have been entrusted with change our attitude and our motivation to give?

_____

_____

_____

_____

Well Done... Additional Food for Thought/Home Study Material

Immediate Gratification vs. Deferred Gratification

One of the greatest challenges for all of us is the tension between immediate gratification and deferred gratification. Over the past few generations there has been a substantial shift from a mindset of deferred gratification to almost an obsession with immediate gratification. There are a number of factors that have contributed to this shift in focus; one of the most notable is the advent of easy credit.

In previous generations, families would scrimp and save in order to make a major purchase, but now with easy credit, people can get it now and pay for it later (with a healthy premium known as interest). The media has also contributed greatly to this immediate gratification thinking, with its never ending enticements claiming that you will never be really happy until you buy this product.

Research confirms that savings among Americans is as low as it has ever been, primarily because after paying for all that has been bought on credit there is little, if anything, left over for saving for the future (deferred gratification).

This scenario is all too common among ordinary people, but is there also an inordinate emphasis on the "here and now" as opposed to the future in the lives of wealthy believers? I think the answer is, "yes." For people of wealth it is not a new phenomenon. Immediate gratification among the rich has been around for centuries.

One of the best examples of this struggle between immediate gratification and deferred gratification can be seen when a rich, young man approaches Jesus about what is necessary to get to Heaven.

> "A ruler questioned Him, saying, 'Good Teacher, what shall I do to inherit eternal life?' And Jesus said to him, 'Why do you call Me good? No one is good except God alone. You know the commandments, Do not commit adultery, Do not murder, Do not steal, Do not bear false witness, Honor your father and mother.' And he said, 'All these things I have kept from my youth.' When Jesus heard this, He said to him, 'One thing you still lack; sell all that you possess and distribute it to the poor, and you shall have treasure in heaven; and come, follow Me." But when he had heard these things, he became very sad, for he was extremely rich." (Luke 18:18-23)

If I were to ask what Jesus is calling for this rich, young ruler to do, virtually everyone would say he is to sell all his possessions, give the proceeds to the poor and follow Jesus – completely skipping over a major point in what He told the young man. Look at the statement again. "One thing you still lack; sell all that you possess and distribute it to the poor, and you shall have treasure in heaven; and come follow Me."

Do you see what we always seem to leave out "and you shall have treasure in heaven." Jesus is not asking this rich young ruler to go and sell all his possessions, give the proceeds to the poor and never see or enjoy them again. Jesus is telling him to trade the temporary immediate gratification of his treasures for the deferred gratification of his treasures for all of eternity. He wasn't asking him to give up anything, He was just calling for him to send it on ahead to be enjoyed later, forever. He was calling this young man to trade immediate gratification for deferred gratification.

The blessings of deferred gratification should not be new to us as Jesus teaches us this same principle in His Sermon on the Mount. "Do not store up for yourselves treasures on earth, where moth and rust destroy, and where thieves break in and steal. But store up for yourselves treasures in heaven, where neither moth nor rust destroys, and where thieves do not break in or steal; for where your treasure is, there your heart will be also." (Matthew 6:19-21)

When we give while we are "on this side of the grass," we may be reducing our earthly net worth, but we are simultaneously increasing our eternal net worth – "you will have treasures in Heaven." These heavenly treasures, whatever exactly they are, will not fluctuate with the rise and fall of the stock market or the economy. They will not be vulnerable to rising or falling interest rates or inflation. We will not need to worry about getting ripped off or making a bad investment choice and maybe losing it all. These heavenly investments that you have sent on ahead are guaranteed by the Creator of the universe – the One who is in control of all things.

Do those of us who have surplus material possessions find ourselves more like the rich, young ruler with an extreme affection for things than we might like to admit? Are we hesitant to sacrificially give today, because of what it might cost us today in reduced current circumstances, financial capacity or earthly security? Do we walk away from opportunities that Jesus sets before us because we are not willing to send some of the earthly wealth that He has entrusted to us on ahead for our future enjoyment?

If we really believed that what we gave was perishable and temporary and would come back to us later and be imperishable and eternally ours, who in their right mind would not gladly trade temporary, immediate gratification for eternal, deferred gratification?

If we want to learn to live by faith, we need to learn to give by faith. How much have you deposited into your heavenly investment account to date? It will be waiting for you.

Well Done... Additional Food for Thought/Home Study Material

Food for Thought Questions

1. How does knowing that "what you give up is perishable and what you get back is imperishab[le]" encourage you?

_____

_____

_____

_____

2. One hundred years from now, how much you accumulated on this earth will be irrelevant and how much you sent on ahead will be yours to enjoy forever. If you really believed this was tru[e], why would you not give everything you could away in this life so you can have it all back in multiples in the next one?

_____

_____

_____

_____

3. If you really believed God at His Word, fully and earnestly, why would we not be willing to do what Jesus asked the rich young ruler to do, if Jesus were to ask us to do the same thing?

_____

_____

_____

_____